FIRST PAST THE POST

Verbal Reasoning:

Practice Papers

Multiple Choice

Book 2

© 2019 ElevenPlusExams.co.uk   COPYING STRICTLY PROHIBITED

How to use this book to make the most of 11 plus exam preparation

It is important to remember that for 11 plus exams there is no national syllabus, no pass mark and no retake option. It is, therefore, vital that your child is fully primed to perform to the best of their ability so that they give themselves the best possible chance on the day.

Unlike similar publications, the **First Past The Post®** series uniquely assesses your child's performance on a question-by-question basis, helping to identify areas for improvement and providing suggestions for further targeted tests. By entering the unique Peer-Compare access code for this book on our website, your child's performance can be compared anonymously to that of others who have taken the same tests.

Verbal Reasoning: Practice Papers

This collection of four timed tests is representative of the standard Verbal Reasoning section of contemporary multi-discipline 11 plus and Common Entrance exams. Each test contains 80 questions and is designed to be completed in 50 minutes. This time is based on classroom testing sessions held at our centre. These tests are especially representative of the Granada Learning (GL) Verbal Reasoning papers but provide useful practice for all exam boards.

Never has it been more useful to learn from mistakes!

Students can improve by as much as 15%, not only by focused practice, but also by targeting any weak areas.

How to manage your child's practice

To get the most up-to-date information, visit our website, www.elevenplusexams.co.uk, the UK's largest online resource for 11 plus, with over 65,000 webpages and a forum administered by a select group of experienced moderators.

About the authors

The Eleven Plus Exams' **First Past The Post®** series has been created by a team of experienced tutors and authors from leading British universities.

Published by Technical One Ltd. t/a Eleven Plus Exams

With special thanks to all the children who tested our material at the ElevenPlusExams centre in Harrow.

ISBN: 978-1-912364-77-0

Copyright © ElevenPlusExams.co.uk 2019

Second edition

elevenplusexams
head for success

All rights reserved. No part of this publication may be reproduced, stored or introduced into a retrieval system or transmitted in any form or by any means, without the prior written permission of the publisher nor may be circulated in any form of binding or cover other than the one in which it was published and without a similar condition including this condition being imposed on the subsequent publisher.

About Us

At Eleven Plus Exams, we supply high-quality 11 plus tuition for your children. Our free website at **www.elevenplusexams.co.uk** is the largest website in the UK that specifically prepares children for the 11 plus exams. We also provide online services to schools and our **First Past The Post®** range of books has been well-received by schools, tuition centres and parents.

Eleven Plus Exams is recognised as a trusted and authoritative source. We have been quoted in numerous national newspapers, including *The Telegraph*, *The Observer*, the *Daily Mail* and *The Sunday Telegraph*, as well as on national television (BBC1 and Channel 4), and BBC radio.

Our website offers a vast amount of information and advice on the 11 plus, including a moderated online forum, books, downloadable material and online services to enhance your child's chances of success. Set up in 2004, the website grew from an initial 20 webpages to more than 65,000 today, and has been visited by millions of parents. It is moderated by experts in the field, who provide support for parents both before and after the exams.

Don't forget to visit **www.elevenplusexams.co.uk** and see why we are the market's leading one-stop shop for all your 11 plus needs. You will find:

- ✓ Comprehensive quality content and advice written by 11 plus experts
- ✓ Eleven Plus Exams online shop supplying a wide range of practice books, e-papers, software and apps
- ✓ Lots of FREE practice papers to download
- ✓ Professional tuition service
- ✓ Short revision courses
- ✓ Year-long 11 plus courses
- ✓ Mock exams tailored to reflect those of the main examining bodies

Other Titles in the First Past The Post® Series
11+ Essentials Range of Books

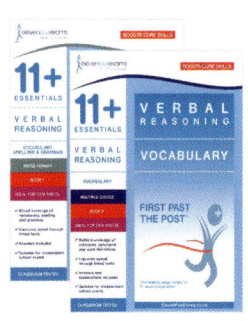

978-1-912364-60-2	Verbal Reasoning: Cloze Tests Book 1 - Mixed Format
978-1-912364-61-9	Verbal Reasoning: Cloze Tests Book 2 - Mixed Format
978-1-912364-78-7	Verbal Reasoning: Cloze Tests Book 3 - Mixed Format
978-1-912364-79-4	Verbal Reasoning: Cloze Tests Book 4 - Mixed Format
978-1-912364-62-6	Verbal Reasoning: Vocabulary Book 1 - Multiple Choice
978-1-912364-63-3	Verbal Reasoning: Vocabulary Book 2 - Multiple Choice
978-1-912364-64-0	Verbal Reasoning: Vocabulary Book 3 - Multiple Choice
978-1-912364-65-7	Verbal Reasoning: Vocabulary, Spelling and Grammar Book 1 - Multiple Choice
978-1-912364-66-4	Verbal Reasoning: Vocabulary, Spelling and Grammar Book 2 - Multiple Choice
978-1-912364-68-8	Verbal Reasoning: Vocabulary in Context Level 1
978-1-912364-69-5	Verbal Reasoning: Vocabulary in Context Level 2
978-1-912364-70-1	Verbal Reasoning: Vocabulary in Context Level 3
978-1-912364-71-8	Verbal Reasoning: Vocabulary in Context Level 4
978-1-912364-74-9	Verbal Reasoning: Vocabulary Puzzles Book 1
978-1-912364-75-6	Verbal Reasoning: Vocabulary Puzzles Book 2
978-1-912364-76-3	Verbal Reasoning: Practice Papers Book 1 - Multiple Choice

978-1-912364-02-2	English: Comprehensions Classic Literature Book 1 - Multiple Choice
978-1-912364-05-3	English: Comprehensions Contemporary Literature Book 1 - Multiple Choice
978-1-912364-08-4	English: Comprehensions Non-Fiction Book 1 - Multiple Choice
978-1-912364-14-5	English: Mini Comprehensions - Inference Book 1
978-1-912364-15-2	English: Mini Comprehensions - Inference Book 2
978-1-912364-16-9	English: Mini Comprehensions - Inference Book 3
978-1-912364-11-4	English: Mini Comprehensions - Fact-Finding Book 1
978-1-912364-12-1	English: Mini Comprehensions - Fact-Finding Book 2
978-1-912364-21-3	English: Spelling, Punctuation and Grammar Book 1
978-1-912364-00-8	English: Practice Papers Book 1 - Multiple Choice
978-1-912364-17-6	Creative Writing Examples

978-1-912364-30-5	Numerical Reasoning: Quick-Fire Book 1
978-1-912364-31-2	Numerical Reasoning: Quick-Fire Book 2
978-1-912364-32-9	Numerical Reasoning: Quick-Fire Book 1 - Multiple Choice
978-1-912364-33-6	Numerical Reasoning: Quick-Fire Book 2 - Multiple Choice
978-1-912364-34-3	Numerical Reasoning: Multi-Part Book 1
978-1-912364-35-0	Numerical Reasoning: Multi-Part Book 2
978-1-912364-36-7	Numerical Reasoning: Multi-Part Book 1 - Multiple Choice
978-1-912364-37-4	Numerical Reasoning: Multi-Part Book 2 - Multiple Choice

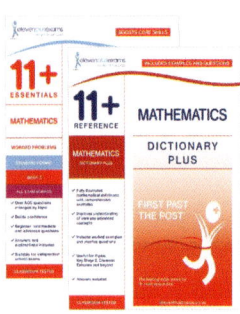

978-1-912364-43-5	Mathematics: Mental Arithmetic Book 1
978-1-912364-44-2	Mathematics: Mental Arithmetic Book 2
978-1-912364-45-9	Mathematics: Worded Problems Book 1
978-1-912364-46-6	Mathematics: Worded Problems Book 2
978-1-912364-52-7	Mathematics: Worded Problems Book 3
978-1-912364-47-3	Mathematics: Dictionary Plus
978-1-912364-50-3	Mathematics: Crossword Puzzles Book 1
978-1-912364-51-0	Mathematics: Crossword Puzzles Book 2
978-1-912364-48-0	Mathematics: Practice Papers Book 1 - Multiple Choice

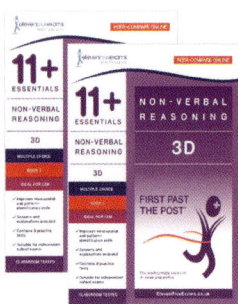

978-1-912364-87-9	Non-Verbal Reasoning: 2D Book 1 - Multiple Choice
978-1-912364-88-6	Non-Verbal Reasoning: 2D Book 2 - Multiple Choice
978-1-912364-85-5	Non-Verbal Reasoning: 3D Book 1 - Multiple Choice
978-1-912364-86-2	Non-Verbal Reasoning: 3D Book 2 - Multiple Choice
978-1-912364-83-1	Non-Verbal Reasoning: Practice Papers Book 1 - Multiple Choice

Contents

Test A	1
Test B	13
Test C	25
Test D	37
Answer Sheets	49
Answers & Explanations	67
Peer-Compare™ access code	inside front cover

This book comprises four tests, each with 80 questions and designed to be completed in 50 minutes. This book also contains the respective answer sheets, answers and explanations for each test.

BLANK PAGE

FIRST PAST THE POST®

VERBAL REASONING

Multiple-Choice

Test A

Read the following instructions carefully:

1) Do not open this test paper until you are told to do so.

2) Please fill in your details accurately at the top of the Answer Sheet.

3) Mark your answer using a **pencil** by drawing a **firm horizontal line** next to your chosen answer on the Answer Sheet.

4) If you want to change your answer, rub out your old answer completely and mark your new answer clearly. You will get no marks for illegible answers.

5) Work as efficiently and carefully as you can to ensure you finish within the time permitted.

6) If you cannot answer a question, go onto the next question; do not waste time.

7) When you have finished a page, go straight onto the next page.

8) When you reach the end, go back to any questions you have missed out and check all your answers.

9) There are **80 questions** and you have **50 minutes** in which to complete this paper.

Good luck!

Copyright © ElevenPlusExams.co.uk 2019

All rights reserved. No part of this publication may be reproduced, stored or introduced into a retrieval system or transmitted in any form or by any means, without the prior written permission of the publisher nor may be circulated in any form of binding or cover other than the one in which it was published and without a similar condition including this condition being imposed on the subsequent publisher.

A B C D E F G H I J K L M N O P Q R S T U V W X Y Z

The alphabet is here to help you with these questions.

Find the next pair of letters in the series and mark it on the answer sheet.

Example   FP   GQ   HR   IS   (??)

Answer   JT

Solution   Both letters in the pair move +1 letter along the alphabet.
Therefore, I + 1 = **J**, and S + 1 = **T**.

1   DH   EI   FJ   GK   (??)

    A HL   **B** IL   **C** GL   **D** HM   **E** IM

2   BY   DW   FU   HS   (??)

    A FR   **B** KQ   **C** FU   **D** JQ   **E** KU

3   MD   JA   GX   DU   (??)

    A AS   **B** BR   **C** AT   **D** BS   **E** AR

4   RJ   SL   TN   UP   (??)

    A VR   **B** BK   **C** PQ   **D** DN   **E** WP

5   CX   DW   FU   IR   (??)

    A MN   **B** NN   **C** MO   **D** MM   **E** NO

6   VG   RJ   NM   JP   (??)

    A FS   **B** TH   **C** BN   **D** RT   **E** JQ

7   PN   KO   FR   AW   (??)

    A VE   **B** UC   **C** WD   **D** VC   **E** VD

PLEASE GO ON TO THE NEXT PAGE

In these questions, find the **two** words, **one** from each group, that will complete the sentence in the best way. Mark **both** words on the answer sheet.

Example   **Kid** is to (child   goat   glove) as **foal** is to (donkey   horse   blanket).

Answer   goat   horse

Solution   In this example, kid is to **goat** as foal is to **horse** is correct because the first word of each pair is the name for the offspring of the second word of each pair.

8 **Chair** is to (stool   furniture   sit) as **hammer** is to (nail   down   tool).

  A stool   X nail
  B furniture   Y down
  C sit   Z tool

9 **Eye** is to (ball   see   two) as **nose** is to (nostril   knows   smell).

  A ball   X nostril
  B see   Y knows
  C two   Z smell

10 **Read** is to (book   dare   study) as **part** is to (only   whole   trap).

  A book   X only
  B dare   Y whole
  C study   Z trap

11 **Bus** is to (transport   wheel   bush) as **bat** is to (night   bath   cricket).

  A transport   X night
  B wheel   Y bath
  C bush   Z cricket

12 **Go** is to (green   went   stop) as **do** is to (does   red   did).

  A green   X does
  B went   Y red
  C stop   Z did

13 **Wash** is to (clean   dry   clothes) as **cut** is to (scissors   strike   pierce).

  A clean   X scissors
  B dry   Y strike
  C clothes   Z pierce

14 **House** is to (chimney   brick   human) as **igloo** is to (snow   straw   deer).

  A chimney   X snow
  B brick   Y straw
  C human   Z deer

PLEASE GO ON TO THE NEXT PAGE

In these questions, the three words in the second group should go together in the **same way** as the three in the first group.

Find the word that is missing in the second group and mark it on the answer sheet.

Example   (croak [cash] shoe)   (males [????] angry)

Answer   mean

Solution   The first and fourth letter of 'males' and first and second letter of 'angry' are put together to make the word '**mean**'.

15   (very [rue] ugly)   (arch [???] aunt)

A tar   B cur   C hat   D car   E cat

16   (until [but] build)   (earth [???] hinge)

A the   B her   C hat   D hit   E get

17   (grind [led] hotel)   (throw [???] regal)

A wet   B low   C wag   D law   E leg

18   (harrow [ham] scream)   (higher [???] stoked)

A hid   B her   C red   D his   E doe

19   (gram [meat] neat)   (bail [????] rush)

A hail   B bush   C bash   D lush   E bars

20   (strife [feat] search)   (ogress [????] winter)

A sing   B rose   C tore   D wing   E grow

21   (fjords [jars] rabbit)   (accord [????] locker)

A coal   B rock   C rack   D race   E cold

PLEASE GO ON TO THE NEXT PAGE

Read the following information, then find the correct answer to the question and mark it on the answer sheet.

22 Rocco is 5 years older than Georgina. Eva is 6 years older than Ben. Georgina is 18 years old. Anita is a year older than Rocco, but a year younger than Ben.

How old is Eva?

A 25
B 26
C 28
D 31
E 33

In these questions, there are two pairs of words. Only **one** of the five possible answers will go equally well with **both** of these pairs. Mark it on the answer sheet.

Example   (globe   planet)   (soil   mud)

Select from (pebble   earth   sand   star   dig)

Answer   earth

23 (rigid   stiff)   (difficult   strenuous)
A board   B hardy   C painful   D heavy   E tough

24 (throw   hurl)   (performers   actors)
A band   B cast   C chuck   D staff   E company

25 (pen   enclosure)   (firm   sturdy)
A field   B hard   C ring   D stable   E cage

26 (tilt   slope)   (thin   haggard)
A slim   B fall   C lean   D slender   E limber

27 (body   torso)   (chest   crate)
A luggage   B hamper   C box   D case   E trunk

28 (curtsy   nod)   (loop   knot)
A lace   B ribbon   C bow   D yield   E salute

29 (lead   manage)   (frank   honest)
A plain   B conduct   C direct   D explicit   E guide

PLEASE GO ON TO THE NEXT PAGE

In these sentences, the words in capitals have both had the same letter taken out. The other letters are then scrambled.

Find the letter that has been taken out of both words.

The sentence that you make must make sense.

Mark the correct letter on the answer sheet.

Example   I **ELI** reading **SOBO**.
Answer   K
Solution   The letter that has been removed from both words is **K**.
The words should be **like** and **books**, as the sentence should read: I like reading books.

30 He swam two **THGSEN** in the **OPO**.

A S   B I   C L   D T   E C

31 She **CEHGSA** her **IMD** quite frequently.

A I   B R   C A   D N   E L

32 I **PYADE** for good exam **USLTSE**.

A L   B M   C E   D R   E H

33 He spent the **OELW** evening **ITW** his parents.

A S   B N   C V   D R   E H

34 **SRFELO** need sunlight to **GOR** well.

A W   B C   C N   D D   E P

35 Some countries **IRVE** on the left **SIE** of the road.

A D   B R   C N   D P   E S

36 She was saving up **EONM** to **UB** a car.

A Y   B R   C C   D D   E N

PLEASE GO ON TO THE NEXT PAGE

In each question, find the number that will complete the sum correctly and mark it on the answer sheet.

Example 26 + 7 = 18 + [?]

Answer 15

Solution The sum on the right must equal the sum on the left. In this case, the calculation on the left equals 33, so the question mark on the right must be replaced by **15**.

37 4 × 3 ÷ 2 = 28 ÷ 4 - [?]

A 1   B 7   C 2   D 4   E 3

38 17 × 4 = 9 × 11 - [?]

A 43   B 63   C 55   D 31   E 49

39 53 + 72 - 36 = 6 × 9 + [?]

A 23   B 39   C 25   D 47   E 35

40 72 ÷ 4 - 3 = 80 ÷ 2 - [?]

A 17   B 25   C 19   D 7   E 15

41 66 ÷ 11 × 6 = 3 × 6 + [?]

A 18   B 36   C 48   D 12   E 24

42 63 ÷ 3 + 29 = 7 × 9 - [?]

A 3   B 30   C 17   D 26   E 13

43 12 × 4 - 7 = 72 ÷ 3 + [?]

A 17   B 27   C 23   D 11   E 15

PLEASE GO ON TO THE NEXT PAGE

In these questions, find **two** words, **one** from each group, that are **most opposite in meaning**.

Mark **both** words on the answer sheet.

Example	(good luck today)	(wish bad charm)
Answer	good bad	
Solution	'Good' means desired or approved of, whereas 'bad' means not hoped for or desired.	

44 (cover   merge   arrange)   (separate   study   discover)

   A cover   X separate
   B merge   Y study
   C arrange   Z discover

45 (success   miracle   safety)   (danger   facade   fear)

   A success   X danger
   B miracle   Y facade
   C safety   Z fear

46 (object   investigate   destroy)   (insert   approve   confirm)

   A object   X insert
   B investigate   Y approve
   C destroy   Z confirm

47 (extend   provoke   classify)   (satisfy   shorten   lengthen)

   A extend   X satisfy
   B provoke   Y shorten
   C classify   Z lengthen

48 (enforce   enlarge   enter)   (force   permit   shrink)

   A enforce   X force
   B enlarge   Y permit
   C enter   Z shrink

49 (menacing   slow   robust)   (hardy   weak   ponderous)

   A menacing   X hardy
   B slow   Y weak
   C robust   Z ponderous

50 (sensitive   healthy   mundane)   (extraordinary   tender   astute)

   A sensitive   X extraordinary
   B healthy   Y tender
   C mundane   Z astute

PLEASE GO ON TO THE NEXT PAGE

In these questions, the **same** letter must fit into **both** sets of brackets, to complete the word in front of the brackets and begin the word after the brackets.

Find this letter and mark it on the answer sheet.

Example	cla [?] ord	cre [?] ipe
Answer	w	
Solution	The same letter that fits into both sets of brackets is '**w**'.	
	The four words are 'cla**w**', '**w**ord', 'cre**w**' and '**w**ipe'.	

51 stin [?] ate   ho [?] rave

A p   B t   C k   D g   E b

52 pec [?] it   thin [?] iss

A h   B g   C e   D k   E m

53 wil [?] ark   lou [?] esk

A m   B d   C e   D t   E c

54 kne [?] ide   stra [?] ake

A p   B r   C b   D w   E d

55 hoo [?] our   whe [?] ilt

A d   B k   C n   D t   E h

56 aren [?] id   ple [?] unt

A p   B s   C a   D b   E d

57 bra [?] ust   brin [?] houl

A m   B g   C e   D d   E t

PLEASE GO ON TO THE NEXT PAGE

In each question, find the number that continues the series in the most sensible way and mark it on the answer sheet.

Example   4   6   8   10   [?]
Answer   12
Solution   This series is formed of consecutive even numbers, and the next term can be found by adding two to the previous term, i.e., 10 + 2 = **12**.

58 5   11   17   23   29   35   [?]
A 42   B 39   C 45   D 41   E 49

59 1   4   9   16   25   [?]
A 41   B 32   C 36   D 34   E 49

60 54   49   57   52   60   [?]
A 67   B 55   C 59   D 68   E 65

61 18   19   21   24   28   [?]
A 31   B 32   C 33   D 34   E 35

62 23   19   22   20   21   21   [?]
A 23   B 20   C 19   D 21   E 18

63 23   20   16   11   [?]
A 3   B 5   C 6   D 9   E 8

64 6   12   9   18   15   [?]
A 24   B 18   C 27   D 30   E 21

65 72   64   69   78   70   75   84   76   [?]
A 83   B 78   C 85   D 87   E 81

Read the following information, then find the correct answer to the question and mark its letter on your answer sheet.

66 In a race, Lewis started off in 6th position. He overtook two other people without being overtaken himself. Fernando then overtook Lewis and one other person to finish the race.

What position does Fernando end up in?

A   1st
B   2nd
C   3rd
D   4th
E   5th

PLEASE GO ON TO THE NEXT PAGE

In these questions, find **two** words, **one** from each group, that make a new word when put together. The order of the letters cannot be changed, and the word from the first group always comes first.

Mark **both** words on the answer sheet.

Example   (hand   finger   toe)   (sum   some   sun)

Answer   hand   some

Solution   The only compound word which can be made from the given choices is '**handsome**'.

67   (deck   gold   ship)   (bird   fish   cat)

    A deck   X bird
    B gold   Y fish
    C ship   Z cat

68   (for   fat   fan)   (give   through   rest)

    A for   X give
    B fat   Y through
    C fan   Z rest

69   (be   star   hat)   (con   cause   leave)

    A be   X con
    B star   Y cause
    C hat   Z leave

70   (come   stand   chest)   (rest   back   slip)

    A come   X rest
    B stand   Y back
    C chest   Z slip

71   (head   stone   sea)   (knot   flow   line)

    A head   X knot
    B stone   Y flow
    C sea   Z line

72   (wind   war   trap)   (blow   let   mill)

    A wind   X blow
    B war   Y let
    C trap   Z mill

73   (white   drop   sand)   (paper   right   eye)

    A white   X paper
    B drop   Y right
    C sand   Z eye

PLEASE GO ON TO THE NEXT PAGE

A B C D E F G H I J K L M N O P Q R S T U V W X Y Z

The alphabet is here to help you with these questions.

Find the letters that complete each sentence in the best way and mark them on the answer sheet.

Example **AB** is to **CD** as **PQ** is to (??).

Answer RS

Solution Both letters in the pair move +2 letters along the alphabet.
Therefore, P + 2 = **R**, and Q + 2 = **S**.

74
HS is to **IT** as **ER** is to (??).

A NO **B** OR **C** FS **D** PS **E** QO

75
XY is to **VW** as **XE** is to (??).

A VY **B** YC **C** VC **D** YF **E** YC

76
CJ is to **GK** as **FW** is to (??).

A JY **B** IY **C** JX **D** IZ **E** IA

77
AC is to **BB** as **PS** is to (??).

A QS **B** RS **C** QT **D** QR **E** RQ

78
BT is to **DO** as **OL** is to (??).

A MQ **B** QM **C** QG **D** QQ **E** MG

79
MP is to **NK** as **RJ** is to (??).

A CD **B** SP **C** GH **D** NH **E** IQ

80
DC is to **WF** as **AD** is to (??).

A ZW **B** SG **C** HH **D** TG **E** ZH

END OF TEST

FIRST PAST THE POST

VERBAL REASONING

Multiple-Choice

Test B

Read the following instructions carefully:

1) Do not open this test paper until you are told to do so.

2) Please fill in your details accurately at the top of the Answer Sheet.

3) Mark your answer using a **pencil** by drawing a **firm horizontal line** next to your chosen answer on the Answer Sheet.

4) If you want to change your answer, rub out your old answer completely and mark your new answer clearly. You will get no marks for illegible answers.

5) Work as efficiently and carefully as you can to ensure you finish within the time permitted.

6) If you cannot answer a question, go onto the next question; do not waste time.

7) When you have finished a page, go straight onto the next page.

8) When you reach the end, go back to any questions you have missed out and check all your answers.

9) There are **80 questions** and you have **50 minutes** in which to complete this paper.

Good luck!

Copyright © ElevenPlusExams.co.uk 2019

All rights reserved. No part of this publication may be reproduced, stored or introduced into a retrieval system or transmitted in any form or by any means, without the prior written permission of the publisher nor may be circulated in any form of binding or cover other than the one in which it was published and without a similar condition including this condition being imposed on the subsequent publisher.

In these questions, letters stand for numbers.

Work out the answer to each sum, then find its letter and mark it on the answer sheet.

Example   If A = 5, B = 14, C = 12, D = 13 and E = 3,
what is the answer to this sum **written as a letter**?

A + C - E = ?

Answer   B

Solution   If we convert the letters into numbers, A + C - E = 5 + 12 - 3 = 14, we can see that B = 14, so the answer to this sum written as a letter is **B**.

1   If A = 3, B = 6, C = 9, D = 21, E = 24,
what is the answer to this sum **written as a letter**?
A + C + A + B

A   A   **B**   B   **C**   C   **D**   D   **E**   E

2   If A = 2, B = 3, C = 9, D = 15, E = 18,
what is the answer to this sum **written as a letter**?
A × D - E + B

A   A   **B**   B   **C**   C   **D**   D   **E**   E

3   If A = 2, B = 4, C = 6, D = 9, E = 12,
what is the answer to this sum **written as a letter**?
B × E ÷ C + B

A   A   **B**   B   **C**   C   **D**   D   **E**   E

4   If A = 1, B = 4, C = 5, D = 6, E = 15,
what is the answer to this sum **written as a letter**?
B × C - E - A

A   A   **B**   B   **C**   C   **D**   D   **E**   E

5   If A = 2, B = 4, C = 12, D = 14, E = 20,
what is the answer to this sum **written as a letter**?
A × D + C - E

A   A   **B**   B   **C**   C   **D**   D   **E**   E

6   If A = 2, B = 3, C = 14, D = 18, E = 24,
what is the answer to this sum **written as a letter**?
D ÷ (B ÷ A) + A

A   A   **B**   B   **C**   C   **D**   D   **E**   E

7   If A = 5, B = 10, C = 15, D = 25, E = 30,
what is the answer to this sum **written as a letter**?
A × C - E - C

A   A   **B**   B   **C**   C   **D**   D   **E**   E

PLEASE GO ON TO THE NEXT PAGE

In each question, one letter can be moved from the first word to the second word to make two new words.

The letters must **not** otherwise be rearranged and **both** new words must make sense.

Find the letter that moves and mark it on the answer sheet.

Example   trick   cat

Answer   r

Solution   Move the letter 'r' from 'trick' to 'cat' to make the new words 'tick' and 'cart'.

8   ghost   thin

A g   B h   C o   D s   E t

9   stone   hat

A s   B t   C o   D n   E e

10 paint   hose

A p   B a   C i   D n   E t

11 hoard   range

A h   B o   C a   D r   E d

12 breach   wing

A b   B r   C e   D a   E c

13 house   vale

A h   B o   C u   D s   E e

14 splash   rice

A s   B p   C l   D a   E h

PLEASE GO ON TO THE NEXT PAGE

A B C D E F G H I J K L M N O P Q R S T U V W X Y Z

The alphabet is here to help you with these questions.

Find the next pair of letters in the series and mark it on the answer sheet.

Example   FP   GQ   HR   IS   (??)

Answer   JT

Solution   Both letters in the pair move +1 letter along the alphabet.
Therefore, I + 1 = **J**, and S + 1 = **T**.

15   YU   ZT   AS   BR   (??)

   A CQ   B CP   C CS   D AQ   E CR

16   EK   AN   WQ   ST   (??)

   A OV   B PW   C SV   D QW   E OW

17   RY   SW   TU   US   (??)

   A FR   B VR   C FQ   D FP   E VQ

18   EQ   KW   QC   WI   (??)

   A DP   B BO   C DN   D CO   E CP

19   YL   TO   OR   JU   (??)

   A DX   B EX   C MP   D EP   E DP

20   YS   DV   IY   NB   (??)

   A RF   B SF   C SG   D SE   E RE

21   RS   KL   DE   WX   (??)

   A QP   B QQ   C RP   D QR   E PQ

22   ET   BX   WB   TF   (??)

   A OK   B PK   C OJ   D PJ   E QK

PLEASE GO ON TO THE NEXT PAGE

Read the following information, then find the correct answer to the question and mark it on the answer sheet.

23 All politicians are crooks. All crooks are liars.
Which one of the following statements must be correct?

A   All politicians are liars.
B   All liars are crooks.
C   All crooks are politicians.
D   All liars are politicians.
E   There are more liars than politicians.

In these sentences, a word of **four letters** is hidden at the **end** of one word and the **beginning** of the next word.

Find the pair of words that contains the hidden word and mark this answer on the answer sheet.

Example   The dog was startled by the noise.

Answer   then

Solution In this sentence, the hidden four-letter word is '**then**', which is made up of the first three letters of the word '**the**' and the first letter of the word '**n**oise'.

24 It's our own brand we're selling.

A It's our   B our own   C own brand   D brand we're   E we're selling.

25 No unicorns have ever actually existed.

A No unicorns   B unicorns have   C have ever   D ever actually   E actually existed.

26 It only lasted for two minutes.

A It only   B only lasted   C lasted for   D for two   E two minutes.

27 I'm asking because we're quite worried.

A I'm asking   B asking because   C because we're   D we're quite   E quite worried.

28 The bystanders ignored my pleas for help.

A The bystanders   B bystanders ignored   C ignored my   D my pleas   E pleas for

29 We called the fire brigade after smelling burning.

A We called   B called the   C the fire   D fire brigade   E brigade after

30 I would much rather be somewhere warmer.

A I would   B would much   C much rather   D rather be   E be somewhere

PLEASE GO ON TO THE NEXT PAGE

In these questions, the missing middle number in the last set is generated in the same way as the middle number in the first two sets. Find the missing number and mark it on the answer sheet.

Example (10 [30] 20)   (6 [18] 12)   (8 [?] 16)

Answer 24

Solution In the first two sets, the middle number is found by adding the two other numbers in the set. Following this pattern, the missing middle number is 8 + 16 = **24**.

31 (31 [50] 19)   (26 [42] 16)   (37 [?] 29)

A 46   B 56   C 72   D 66   E 71

32 (54 [9] 6)   (72 [12] 6)   (45 [?] 5)

A 5   B 4   C 6   D 9   E 8

33 (4 [24] 6)   (14 [168] 12)   (13 [?] 12)

A 156   B 152   C 144   D 148   E 132

34 (4 [22] 15)   (11 [28] 25)   (39 [?] 56)

A 14   B 46   C 17   D 29   E 34

35 (4 [53] 13)   (5 [31] 6)   (6 [?] 16)

A 105   B 97   C 113   D 96   E 73

36 (24 [32] 20)   (120 [66] 6)   (36 [?] 75)

A 93   B 98   C 87   D 84   E 111

37 (12 [53] 29)   (7 [20] 6)   (12 [?] 84)

A 64   B 72   C 84   D 96   E 108

Read the following information, then find the correct answer to the question and mark it on the answer sheet.

38 The day after tomorrow is Wednesday.

What day was it 3 days ago?

A Tuesday
B Saturday
C Friday
D Thursday
E Sunday

PLEASE GO ON TO THE NEXT PAGE

In these questions, three of the five words are related in some way.

Find the **two** words that do not go with these three and mark them **both** on the answer sheet.

Example   red   white   pole   blue   flag

Answer   **pole   flag**

Solution   The words 'red', 'white' and 'blue' are related because they are all colours. The words '**pole**' and '**flag**' do not go with these three words.

39   orchid   blue   elm   rose   daisy

A orchid   B blue   C elm   D rose   E daisy

40   know   eye   sight   sound   taste

A know   B eye   C sight   D sound   E taste

41   collect   spend   gather   save   exchange

A collect   B spend   C gather   D save   E exchange

42   lounge   floor   kitchen   bedroom   house

A lounge   B floor   C kitchen   D bedroom   E house

43   direct   blunt   round   honest   sharp

A direct   B blunt   C round   D honest   E sharp

44   cousin   uncle   grandson   nephew   child

A cousin   B uncle   C grandson   D nephew   E child

45   fast   rapid   speed   brisk   slow

A fast   B rapid   C speed   D brisk   E slow

PLEASE GO ON TO THE NEXT PAGE

A B C D E F G H I J K L M N O P Q R S T U V W X Y Z

The alphabet is here to help you with these questions.

In each of these questions, the code is different. Find the answer to each question and mark it on the answer sheet.

Example   If the code for **EXAM** is **FYBN**, what does **HPPE** mean?

Answer   **GOOD**

Solution   In the word 'EXAM', each letter moves + 1 letter along the alphabet to make the code 'FYBN'. Therefore, each letter in the code 'HPPE' must move - 1 letter along the alphabet to make the word '**GOOD**'.

46 If **FTKK** is the code for **GULL**, what is the code for **CAKE**?

A AZJD   B BZJD   C AZLD   D ACJD   E BZLD

47 If **LIST** is written in code as **NKUV**, what word is written as **NKEM** in code?

A LICK   B LEAK   C LOCK   D LIST   E LATE

48 If **CHNM** is the code for **YELL**, what is the code for **FIRE**?

A JPTF   B JLTF   C IPUF   D IPTI   E JPUI

49 If **YOLG** is the code for **BLOT**, what word is written as **SVZO** in code?

A PARK   B VENT   C BASK   D HEAL   E LUSH

50 If **ROPE** is written in code as **QPOF**, what is the code for **FLAT**?

A GMBU   B EKZU   C EMBS   D GKZS   E EMZU

51 If **DRAB** is the code for **CUFF**, what word is written as **PLUA** in code?

A RAMP   B RICE   C POSE   D OOZE   E QUIT

52 If **COMB** is written in code as **DLOY**, what is the code for **THAT**?

A SECQ   B SIBS   C SEBQ   D UECQ   E UIBS

PLEASE GO ON TO THE NEXT PAGE

In these questions, find **two** words, **one** from each group, that are **closest in meaning**.

Mark **both** words on the answer sheet.

Example   (cheap   expensive   bargain)   (poor   ordinary   inexpensive)

Answer   **cheap   inexpensive**

Solution   Both '**cheap**' and '**inexpensive**' mean low in price.

53 (greedy   angry   weary)   (joyous   tired   miserable)

A greedy   B angry   C weary   X joyous   Y tired   Z miserable

54 (touch   hit   lean)   (bounce   strike   fall)

A touch   B hit   C lean   X bounce   Y strike   Z fall

55 (throw   transfer   give)   (spend   carry   place)

A throw   B transfer   C give   X spend   Y carry   Z place

56 (firm   office   branch)   (produce   stiff   factory)

A firm   B office   C branch   X produce   Y stiff   Z factory

57 (understand   relief   pursue)   (chase   believe   explain)

A understand   B relief   C pursue   X chase   Y believe   Z explain

58 (decide   collide   disturb)   (interrupt   collapse   demise)

A decide   B collide   C disturb   X interrupt   Y collapse   Z demise

59 (mystical   morose   turgid)   (cryptic   multiple   sullen)

A mystical   B morose   C turgid   X cryptic   Y multiple   Z sullen

PLEASE GO ON TO THE NEXT PAGE

In these questions, the **same** letter must fit into **both** sets of brackets, to complete the word in front of the brackets and begin the word after the brackets.

Find this letter and mark it on the answer sheet.

Example   cla [?] ord   cre [?] ipe

Answer   w

Solution   The same letter that fits into both sets of brackets is '**w**'.
                   The four words are 'cla**w**', '**w**ord', 'cre**w**' and '**w**ipe'.

60   toot [?] ind   mas [?] ead

   A s   **B** b   **C** f   **D** h   **E** l

61   pas [?] oup   her [?] eek

   A h   **B** b   **C** l   **D** d   **E** s

62   sal [?] nd   bar [?] yes

   A a   **B** n   **C** e   **D** o   **E** t

63   bu [?] rid   sin [?] as

   A g   **B** s   **C** b   **D** h   **E** t

64   see [?] est   whe [?] ose

   A n   **B** r   **C** d   **D** h   **E** t

65   sli [?] ail   pan [?] alk

   A m   **B** d   **C** w   **D** b   **E** t

66   sul [?] iln   ris [?] not

   A c   **B** g   **C** k   **D** z   **E** s

67   bri [?] aid   drea [?] ore

   A b   **B** m   **C** e   **D** d   **E** g

PLEASE GO ON TO THE NEXT PAGE

Three of these four words are given in code. The codes are **not** written in the same order as the words and one code is missing. Choose the correct answer and mark it on the answer sheet.

SLAP   PASS   WILL   HALT

1046   3944   2405

68 Find the code for the word **SLAP**.

A 2405   B 1046   C 3945   D 2905   E 3944

69 Find the word that has the number code **5032**.

A SLIP   B SWAP   C PAIL   D HAIL   E PAWS

70 Find the code for the word **SHALL**.

A 32400   B 31044   C 12400   D 23844   E 21044

Three of these four words are given in code. The codes are **not** written in the same order as the words and one code is missing. Choose the correct answer and mark it on the answer sheet.

SING   WRAP   SPAN   PANT

3275   9861   1674

71 Find the word that has the number code **9861**.

A WRAP   B SING   C PAST   D SPAN   E SPAWN

72 Find the code for the word **SPAN**.

A 1674   B 9861   C 3275   D 9374   E 3167

73 Find the word that has the number code **8674275**.

A PARSNIP B AGAINST C RANTING D WAITING E WANTING

PLEASE GO ON TO THE NEXT PAGE

In these sentences, the word in capitals has had three letters next to each other taken out.

These three letters will make one correctly-spelt word without changing their order.

The sentence that you make must make sense.

Mark the correct three letter word on the answer sheet.

Example   The children **GATED** in the hall.

Answer   **HER**

Solution   The three letter word that has been removed from 'GATED' is '**HER**'. If we place this three letter word between 'T' and 'E', it makes the word 'GAT**HER**ED', which completes the sentence.

74 People often **FOR** where they put things.

A SAT   B GET   C MAT   D BED   E GOT

75 We had a **CONVERION** about what to do.

A THE   B BAT   C HOT   D SAT   E SHE

76 The house was **DAMD** by the flood.

A PER   B PEN   C AGE   D ARE   E AID

77 He was wearing a shirt and long **TRORS**.

A MEN   B USE   C BAT   D SEA   E EAR

78 She looked **EANT** in her new dress.

A LEG   B PET   C MAN   D MEN   E BET

79 I sat **WEEN** the two seats.

A SHE   B FOR   C BET   D SIT   E LAB

80 I was **OINALLY** going to do it myself.

A SIN   B RIG   C OPT   D PIN   E LET

END OF TEST

FIRST PAST THE POST

VERBAL REASONING

Multiple-Choice

Test C

Read the following instructions carefully:

1) Do not open this test paper until you are told to do so.

2) Please fill in your details accurately at the top of the Answer Sheet.

3) Mark your answer using a **pencil** by drawing a **firm horizontal line** next to your chosen answer on the Answer Sheet.

4) If you want to change your answer, rub out your old answer completely and mark your new answer clearly. You will get no marks for illegible answers.

5) Work as efficiently and carefully as you can to ensure you finish within the time permitted.

6) If you cannot answer a question, go onto the next question; do not waste time.

7) When you have finished a page, go straight onto the next page.

8) When you reach the end, go back to any questions you have missed out and check all your answers.

9) There are **80 questions** and you have **50 minutes** in which to complete this paper.

Good luck!

Copyright © ElevenPlusExams.co.uk 2019

All rights reserved. No part of this publication may be reproduced, stored or introduced into a retrieval system or transmitted in any form or by any means, without the prior written permission of the publisher nor may be circulated in any form of binding or cover other than the one in which it was published and without a similar condition including this condition being imposed on the subsequent publisher.

In each question, one letter can be moved from the first word to the second word to make two new words.

The letters must **not** otherwise be rearranged and **both** new words must make sense.

Find the letter that moves and mark it on the answer sheet.

Example	trick	cat
Answer	r	
Solution	Move the letter 'r' from 'trick' to 'cat' to make the new words 'tick' and 'cart'.	

1 shock   mats

A s   B h   C o   D c   E k

2 beach   read

A b   B e   C a   D c   E h

3 honey   earn

A h   B o   C n   D e   E y

4 shift   toot

A s   B h   C i   D f   E t

5 planet   very

A p   B l   C n   D e   E t

6 brown   sake

A b   B r   C o   D w   E n

7 force   rest

A f   B o   C r   D c   E e

PLEASE GO ON TO THE NEXT PAGE

In each question, find the number that continues the series in the most sensible way and mark it on the answer sheet.

Example   4   6   8   10   [?]

Answer   12

Solution   This series is formed of consecutive even numbers, and the next term can be found by adding two to the previous term, i.e., 10 + 2 = **12**.

8   28   35   42   49   56   [?]

  A 59   **B** 61   **C** 69   **D** 63   **E** 65

9   24   22   18   16   12   [?]

  A 9   **B** 8   **C** 6   **D** 10   **E** 4

10   17   18   20   24   32   [?]

  A 38   **B** 48   **C** 36   **D** 33   **E** 42

11   13   19   35   41   57   63   [?]

  A 79   **B** 84   **C** 74   **D** 69   **E** 89

12   1   8   27   64   [?]

  A 192   **B** 169   **C** 144   **D** 125   **E** 100

13   3   7   10   17   27   44   [?]

  A 71   **B** 75   **C** 61   **D** 54   **E** 65

14   15   12   18   24   21   48   [?]

  A 45   **B** 96   **C** 24   **D** 42   **E** 51

PLEASE GO ON TO THE NEXT PAGE

In these questions, find **two** words, **one** from each group, that are **most opposite in meaning**.

Mark **both** words on the answer sheet.

Example   (good   luck   today)   (wish   bad   charm)

Answer   good   bad

Solution   'Good' means desired or approved of, whereas 'bad' means not hoped for or desired.

15   (upload   pressure   survive)   (inform   perish   delete)

A upload   B pressure   C survive   X inform   Y perish   Z delete

16   (emotional   gigantic   friendly)   (ambitious   quiet   hostile)

A emotional   B gigantic   C friendly   X ambitious   Y quiet   Z hostile

17   (gift   perpetual   absent)   (present   gradual   vague)

A gift   B perpetual   C absent   X present   Y gradual   Z vague

18   (illegal   vulgar   legendary)   (lawful   chaotic   neutral)

A illegal   B vulgar   C legendary   X lawful   Y chaotic   Z neutral

19   (senseless   vain   fighter)   (eager   modest   power)

A senseless   B vain   C fighter   X eager   Y modest   Z power

20   (exotic   remote   winding)   (mobile   nearby   convenient)

A exotic   B remote   C winding   X mobile   Y nearby   Z convenient

21   (redundant   useless   involved)   (complex   complete   employed)

A redundant   B useless   C involved   X complex   Y complete   Z employed

---

Read the following information, then find the correct answer to the question and mark it on the answer sheet.

22   Sports classes are offered on a seasonal basis. Tennis is offered from April to September. Football is offered in all months with exactly 31 days. Rugby is offered from September to December, and from March to May. Ice Hockey is offered from October to March, and also in May. Lacrosse is offered from March to May, and also from August to September.

Which sport is offered for the least number of months?

A   Tennis
B   Football
C   Rugby
D   Ice Hockey
E   Lacrosse

PLEASE GO ON TO THE NEXT PAGE

In these questions, the three words in the second group should go together in the **same way** as the three in the first group.

Find the word that is missing in the second group and mark it on the answer sheet.

Example	(croak [cash] shoe)	(males [????] angry)
Answer	mean	
Solution	The first and fourth letter of 'males' and first and second letter of 'angry' are put together to make the word '**mean**'.	

23 (bread [pea] apple)   (cleft [???] tower)

    A owe   B let   C few   D lot   E wet

24 (brick [lab] flash)   (drive [???] skill)

    A lie   B rid   C led   D kid   E die

25 (whip [what] that)   (star [????] them)

    A sham   B meat   C hart   D stem   E sear

26 (grout [hour] heard)   (steal [????] flick)

    A fast   B fate   C sick   D feat   E salt

27 (curdle [red] sunset)   (duster [???] thawed)

    A wed   B set   C wet   D sew   E she

28 (poodle [pad] almond)   (conned [???] action)

    A one   B cat   C nod   D act   E can

29 (warmup [rear] candle)   (retina [????] lavish)

    A that   B seal   C seat   D tint   E teal

PLEASE GO ON TO THE NEXT PAGE

In these sentences, a word of **four letters** is hidden at the **end** of one word and the **beginning** of the next word.

Find the pair of words that contains the hidden word and mark this answer on the answer sheet.

Example   The dog was startled by the noise.

Answer   then

Solution   In this sentence, the hidden four-letter word is '**then**', which is made up of the first three letters of the word '**the**' and the first letter of the word '**n**oise'.

30 She took the day off ill.

A She took   B took the   C the day   D day off   E off ill.

31 Friendly people like engaging in conversations.

A Friendly people   B people like   C like engaging   D engaging in   E in conversations.

32 Children grow ashamed of their parents.

A Children grow   B grow ashamed   C ashamed of   D of their   E their parents.

33 He's older than he might look.

A He's older   B older than   C than he   D he might   E might look.

34 It meant something was very wrong.

A It meant   B meant something   C something was   D was very   E very wrong.

35 Dogs still impress me when they do tricks.

A Dogs still   B still impress   C impress me   D me when   E when they

36 A crescent moon lit up the sky.

A A crescent   B crescent moon   C moon lit   D lit up   E up the

PLEASE GO ON TO THE NEXT PAGE

In these questions, letters stand for numbers.

Work out the answer to each sum, then find its letter and mark it on the answer sheet.

Example If A = 5, B = 14, C = 12, D = 13 and E = 3,
what is the answer to this sum **written as a letter**?

A + C - E = ?

Answer B

Solution If we convert the letters into numbers, A + C - E = 5 + 12 - 3 = 14, we can see that B = 14, so the answer to this sum written as a letter is **B**.

37 If A = 3, B = 6, C = 9, D = 10, E = 12,
what is the answer to this sum **written as a letter**?
C ÷ A + E - B

A A **B** B **C** C **D** D **E** E

38 If A = 3, B = 8, C = 9, D = 15, E = 72,
what is the answer to this sum **written as a letter**?
E ÷ A ÷ B

A A **B** B **C** C **D** D **E** E

39 If A = 1, B = 6, C = 8, D = 11, E = 12,
what is the answer to this sum **written as a letter**?
D × E ÷ B - D

A A **B** B **C** C **D** D **E** E

40 If A = 4, B = 7, C = 27, D = 42, E = 63,
what is the answer to this sum **written as a letter**?
E ÷ B × A + C

A A **B** B **C** C **D** D **E** E

41 If A = 4, B = 5, C = 8, D = 10, E = 18,
what is the answer to this sum **written as a letter**?
A × B + C - E

A A **B** B **C** C **D** D **E** E

42 If A = 3, B = 4, C = 16, D = 24, E = 30,
what is the answer to this sum **written as a letter**?
E ÷ A + D - B

A A **B** B **C** C **D** D **E** E

43 If A = 2, B = 3, C = 5, D = 9, E = 27,
what is the answer to this sum **written as a letter**?
A × C × B - E

A A **B** B **C** C **D** D **E** E

PLEASE GO ON TO THE NEXT PAGE

In these questions, the **same** letter must fit into **both** sets of brackets, to complete the word in front of the brackets and begin the word after the brackets.

Find this letter and mark it on the answer sheet.

Example   cla [?] ord   cre [?] ipe

Answer   w

Solution   The same letter that fits into both sets of brackets is '**w**'.
The four words are 'cla**w**', '**w**ord', 'cre**w**' and '**w**ipe'.

44 glas [?] oul   fur [?] elf

  A m   B e   C s   D l   E f

45 show [?] ewt   whe [?] igh

  A s   B t   C d   D n   E h

46 cam [?] ost   sho [?] ull

  A m   B p   C k   D h   E d

47 gu [?] ilk   swa [?] ain

  A n   B t   C m   D p   E l

48 win [?] uel   bon [?] ent

  A m   B e   C k   D s   E d

49 sou [?] asp   pai [?] aid

  A l   B s   C r   D p   E n

50 te [?] im   dram [?] rid

  A r   B d   C g   D p   E a

PLEASE GO ON TO THE NEXT PAGE

A B C D E F G H I J K L M N O P Q R S T U V W X Y Z

The alphabet is here to help you with these questions.

In each of these questions, the code is different. Find the answer to each question and mark it on the answer sheet.

Example   If the code for **EXAM** is **FYBN**, what does **HPPE** mean?

Answer   **GOOD**

Solution   In the word 'EXAM', each letter moves + 1 letter along the alphabet to make the code 'FYBN'. Therefore, each letter in the code 'HPPE' must move - 1 letter along the alphabet to make the word '**GOOD**'.

51 If **EQKP** is the code for **COIN**, what word is written as **ITCD** in code?

  A HART   B GRAB   C KING   D GROW   E HOME

52 If **DEAL** is written in code as **BCYJ**, what is the code for **YEAR**?

  A ZBCQ   B AGCT   C WCYP   D VBZQ   E WGCT

53 If **UZPV** is the code for **FAKE**, what word is written as **TLOW** in code?

  A BARK   B LEAD   C BANK   D GOLD   E SICK

54 If **OCWJ** is the code for **SEAL**, what word is written as **CYIC** in code?

  A TAME   B GOAL   C THAN   D FOLD   E GAME

55 If **TVDV** is the code for **STAR**, what is the code for **EAST**?

  A FBSR   B FCVX   C DYSS   D FBWY   E DEXA

56 If **OVER** is written in code as **PXHV**, what is the code for **LIFE**?

  A MKII   B NKIJ   C MKIJ   D MLII   E NLIJ

57 If **RASP** is written in code as **MYNR**, what word is written as **NYGG** in code?

  A SOLE   B HALT   C TIME   D SALE   E SHOE

PLEASE GO ON TO THE NEXT PAGE

In these questions, three of the five words are related in some way.

Find the **two** words that do not go with these three and mark them **both** on the answer sheet.

Example   red   white   pole   blue   flag

Answer   **pole, flag**

58 right   sad   left   correct   down

A right   B sad   C left   D correct   E down

59 star   lamp   stone   candle   shine

A star   B lamp   C stone   D candle   E shine

60 damage   medicine   harm   bandage   injure

A damage   B medicine   C harm   D bandage   E injure

61 bitter   sweet   taste   sour   food

A bitter   B sweet   C taste   D sour   E food

62 flour   salt   mustard   bread   vinegar

A flour   B salt   C mustard   D bread   E vinegar

63 journey   fall   trip   destination   voyage

A journey   B fall   C trip   D destination   E voyage

64 season   winter   autumn   cold   spring

A season   B winter   C autumn   D cold   E spring

65 complete   retire   total   finish   entire

A complete   B retire   C total   D finish   E entire

Read the following information, then find the correct answer to the question and mark it on the answer sheet.

66 Oranges and lemons are citrus fruits. Oranges are sold in bags of 5. Lemons are sold in bags of 6. Beth buys an equal number of bags of oranges as bags of lemons.

Which of the following statements must be true?

A Beth has bought an even number of citrus fruits.

B Beth has bought more lemons than oranges.

C Beth has bought more than 20 citrus fruits.

D Beth has bought more oranges than lemons.

E Beth likes lemons more than oranges.

PLEASE GO ON TO THE NEXT PAGE

In these questions, find the **two** words, **one** from each group, that will complete the sentence in the best way. Mark **both** words on the answer sheet.

Example   **Kid** is to (child   goat   glove) as **foal** is to (donkey   horse   blanket).

Answer   goat   horse

Solution   In this example, kid is to **goat** as foal is to **horse** is correct because the first word of each pair is the name for the offspring of the second word of each pair.

67 **Meat** is to (meet   savoury   vegetable) as **lemon** is to (fruit   sour   melon).

- A meet
- B savoury
- C vegetable
- X fruit
- Y sour
- Z melon

68 **Prince** is to (king   rule   princess) as **ram** is to (doe   horns   ewe).

- A king
- B rule
- C princess
- X doe
- Y horns
- Z ewe

69 **Balloon** is to (round   air   party) as **bottle** is to (water   carry   sports).

- A round
- B air
- C party
- X water
- Y carry
- Z sports

70 **Gram** is to (scales   kilogram   flour) as **litre** is to (water   capacity   metric).

- A scales
- B kilogram
- C flour
- X water
- Y capacity
- Z metric

71 **Fish** is to (scale   swim   school) as **birds** is to (song   robin   flock).

- A scale
- B swim
- C school
- X song
- Y robin
- Z flock

72 **North** is to (up   south   compass) as **outside** is to (sports   within   internal).

- A up
- B south
- C compass
- X sports
- Y within
- Z internal

73 **Nail** is to (hammer   finger   attach) as **bolt** is to (key   lightning   spanner).

- A hammer
- B finger
- C attach
- X key
- Y lightning
- Z spanner

PLEASE GO ON TO THE NEXT PAGE

A B C D E F G H I J K L M N O P Q R S T U V W X Y Z

The alphabet is here to help you with these questions.

Find the letters that complete each sentence in the best way and mark them on the answer sheet.

Example   **AB** is to **CD** as **PQ** is to (??).

Answer   **RS**

Solution   Both letters in the pair move +2 letters along the alphabet.
Therefore, P + 2 = **R**, and Q + 2 = **S**.

74   TF is to VG as EM is to (??).

  A HN   **B** GM   **C** GO   **D** HM   **E** GN

75   OM is to NL as BQ is to (??).

  A AQ   **B** CQ   **C** CD   **D** CR   **E** AP

76   SL is to UN as II is to (??).

  A MK   **B** KL   **C** KN   **D** KK   **E** LK

77   QK is to RH as ZG is to (??).

  A AC   **B** BD   **C** AD   **D** AE   **E** CA

78   GY is to JT as UF is to (??).

  A YL   **B** XL   **C** YM   **D** XA   **E** XM

79   IJ is to MO as NQ is to (??).

  A TJ   **B** TB   **C** SV   **D** EJ   **E** RV

80   PG is to WJ as DR is to (??).

  A KU   **B** KR   **C** HU   **D** IU   **E** HR

END OF TEST

FIRST PAST THE POST

VERBAL REASONING

Multiple-Choice

Test D

Read the following instructions carefully:

1) Do not open this test paper until you are told to do so.

2) Please fill in your details accurately at the top of the Answer Sheet.

3) Mark your answer using a **pencil** by drawing a **firm horizontal line** next to your chosen answer on the Answer Sheet.

4) If you want to change your answer, rub out your old answer completely and mark your new answer clearly. You will get no marks for illegible answers.

5) Work as efficiently and carefully as you can to ensure you finish within the time permitted.

6) If you cannot answer a question, go onto the next question; do not waste time.

7) When you have finished a page, go straight onto the next page.

8) When you reach the end, go back to any questions you have missed out and check all your answers.

9) There are **80 questions** and you have **50 minutes** in which to complete this paper.

Good luck!

Copyright © ElevenPlusExams.co.uk 2019

All rights reserved. No part of this publication may be reproduced, stored or introduced into a retrieval system or transmitted in any form or by any means, without the prior written permission of the publisher nor may be circulated in any form of binding or cover other than the one in which it was published and without a similar condition including this condition being imposed on the subsequent publisher.

In each question, find the number that will complete the sum correctly and mark it on the answer sheet.

Example   26 + 7 = 18 + [?]

Answer   15

Solution   The sum on the right must equal the sum on the left. In this case, the calculation on the left equals 33, so the question mark on the right must be replaced by **15**.

1 13 × 4 × 3 = 3 × 2 × [?]

  A 26   **B** 17   **C** 28   **D** 13   **E** 23

2 81 ÷ 27 + 15 = 17 + 5 - [?]

  A 4   **B** 9   **C** 2   **D** 19   **E** 12

3 24 + 23 - 35 = 5 × 6 - [?]

  A 16   **B** 18   **C** 23   **D** 11   **E** 15

4 8 × 3 + 36 = 13 × 5 - [?]

  A 25   **B** 18   **C** 5   **D** 9   **E** 15

5 15 × 7 - 25 = 8 × 8 + [?]

  A 36   **B** 6   **C** 46   **D** 26   **E** 16

6 13 × 12 - 99 = 14 × 10 - [?]

  A 83   **B** 84   **C** 81   **D** 73   **E** 71

7 75 - 17 - 19 = 6 × 7 - [?]

  A 8   **B** 3   **C** 18   **D** 15   **E** 11

PLEASE GO ON TO THE NEXT PAGE

In these questions, find **two** words, **one** from each group, that make a new word when put together. The order of the letters cannot be changed, and the word from the first group always comes first.

Mark **both** words on the answer sheet.

Example   (hand   finger   toe)   (sum   some   sun)

Answer   hand   some

Solution   The only compound word which can be made from the given choices is '**handsome**'.

8   (cold   fill   drag)   (search   on   card)
- A cold
- B fill
- C drag
- X search
- Y on
- Z card

9   (must   par   further)   (send   more   rat)
- A must
- B par
- C further
- X send
- Y more
- Z rat

10 (for   pick   under)   (pocket   tie   shoe)
- A for
- B pick
- C under
- X pocket
- Y tie
- Z shoe

11 (take   rain   water)   (rise   sing   forest)
- A take
- B rain
- C water
- X ring
- Y sing
- Z forest

12 (rat   more   draw)   (her   rage   grid)
- A rat
- B more
- C draw
- X her
- Y rage
- Z grid

13 (rain   pea   brow)   (skill   sing   skin)
- A rain
- B pea
- C brow
- X skill
- Y sing
- Z skin

14 (tag   man   bud)   (park   get   mask)
- A tag
- B man
- C bud
- X park
- Y get
- Z mask

PLEASE GO ON TO THE NEXT PAGE

In these sentences, the word in capitals has had three letters next to each other taken out.

These three letters will make one correctly-spelt word without changing their order.

The sentence that you make must make sense.

Mark the correct three letter word on the answer sheet.

Example   The children **GATED** in the hall.

Answer   **HER**

Solution   The three letter word that has been removed from 'GATED' is '**HER**'. If we place this three letter word between 'T' and 'E', it makes the word 'GAT**HER**ED', which completes the sentence.

15 I will see you again next **FAY**.

   A LAG   **B** RID   **C** INN   **D** AND   **E** DAY

16 She walked **EFOOT** on the beach.

   A RED   **B** BAR   **C** NOT   **D** ACT   **E** CON

17 The road was **SPERY** due to the ice.

   A LIP   **B** PIN   **C** TAP   **D** ATE   **E** AND

18 It is the **SEA** for celebration.

   A CAR   **B** MAN   **C** BED   **D** POT   **E** SON

19 He had to sing on **SE**.

   A SET   **B** RAT   **C** SEW   **D** PIN   **E** TAG

20 The town hall lies to the **SH** of the church.

   A ALL   **B** ART   **C** OUT   **D** ARC   **E** USE

21 It takes a lot of **IENCE** to be a nurse.

   A BUT   **B** CON   **C** SIX   **D** PAT   **E** PEN

22 You could reach it using a **LER**.

   A RUE   **B** ADD   **C** BAT   **D** ANT   **E** TEA

PLEASE GO ON TO THE NEXT PAGE

Read the following information, then find the correct answer to the question and mark it on the answer sheet.

23 Romera speaks Spanish and Portuguese. Craig speaks English and German. Gene speaks Italian, French and Greek. Fatima only speaks German. Merida speaks English and French.

Which person cannot communicate with any of the others?

A Romera

B Craig

C Gene

D Fatima

E Merida

In these questions, find two words, one from each group, that are closest in meaning.

Mark both words on the answer sheet.

Example   (cheap   expensive   bargain)   (poor   ordinary   inexpensive)

Answer   cheap   inexpensive

Solution   Both 'cheap' and 'inexpensive' mean low in price.

24 (introduce   drive   regret)   (terminate   suffer   launch)

A introduce   B drive   C regret   X terminate   Y suffer   Z launch

25 (grateful   unlikely   fortunate)   (lucky   tricky   stocky)

A grateful   B unlikely   C fortunate   X lucky   Y tricky   Z stocky

26 (remember   murmur   confuse)   (mumble   feeble   tremble)

A remember   B murmur   C confuse   X mumble   Y feeble   Z tremble

27 (question   ponder   wonder)   (consider   panic   answer)

A question   B ponder   C wonder   X consider   Y panic   Z answer

28 (hardy   strict   zealous)   (arrogant   direct   enthusiastic)

A hardy   B strict   C zealous   X arrogant   Y direct   Z enthusiastic

29 (loop   string   stick)   (chain   coil   pin)

A loop   B string   C stick   X chain   Y coil   Z pin

30 (shy   fragile   unusual)   (muddled   curious   brave)

A shy   B fragile   C unusual   X muddled   Y curious   Z brave

PLEASE GO ON TO THE NEXT PAGE

In each question, one letter can be moved from the first word to the second word to make two new words.

The letters must **not** otherwise be rearranged and **both** new words must make sense.

Find the letter that moves and mark it on the answer sheet.

Example	trick	cat
Answer	r	
Solution	Move the letter 'r' from 'trick' to 'cat' to make the new words 'tick' and 'cart'.	

31 wrung   heat

A w   B r   C u   D n   E g

32 grate   rain

A g   B r   C a   D t   E e

33 heart   sage

A h   B e   C a   D r   E t

34 bound   bogs

A b   B o   C u   D n   E d

35 hoist   coped

A h   B o   C i   D s   E t

36 chart   cave

A c   B h   C a   D r   E t

37 shove   seen

A s   B h   C o   D v   E e

PLEASE GO ON TO THE NEXT PAGE

Three of these four words are given in code. The codes are **not** written in the same order as the words and one code is missing. Choose the correct answer and mark it on the answer sheet.

PULP   BEAN   SOBS   JUST

8370   5285   1954

38   Find the code for the word **JUST**.

A 7362   B 8370   C 5285   D 1954   E 6284

39   Find the word that has the number code **87012**.

A BANJO   B BATON   C SETUP   D BEANS   E PLEAT

40   Find the code for the word **BOAST**.

A 82754   B 52689   C 12705   D 81270   E 56982

Three of these four words are given in code. The codes are **not** written in the same order as the words and one code is missing. Choose the correct answer and mark it on the answer sheet.

PART   SPIN   REAR   TRAP

9351   3753   4128

41   Find the code for the word **PART**.

A 9351   B 1539   C 9531   D 3753   E 3486

42   Find the word that has the number code **41237**.

A SPEAR   B SPIRE   C PASTE   D PINES   E TRAIN

43   Find the code for the word **RATE**.

A 9537   B 3519   C 9413   D 4873   E 3597

PLEASE GO ON TO THE NEXT PAGE

In these questions, the second word in the last set is made up in the same way as the second words in the first two sets.

Find the missing word and mark it on the answer sheet.

Example (cheat heat) (tread read) (shoot [????])

Answer **hoot**

Solution In the first two sets, the first letter of the first word has been removed to make the second word. Following this pattern, the missing word in the last set is '**hoot**'.

44 (grass grow) (steal stow) (snake [????])

  A snow B know C stow D sow E now

45 (blank bank) (cease case) (scold [????])

  A cold B sold C cods D clod E olds

46 (these the) (faint fat) (bacon [???])

  A ban B nob C cab D cob E nab

47 (relate tale) (regard rage) (metals [????])

  A meal B tame C late D teal E mate

48 (blast tab) (prior rip) (draws [???])

  A raw B was C sad D war E saw

49 (apple pea) (heads ash) (drawn [???])

  A war B and C raw D wan E awn

50 (aware wear) (spite pest) (ample [????])

  A lame B male C pale D plea E meal

PLEASE GO ON TO THE NEXT PAGE

In these questions, the missing middle number in the last set is generated in the same way as the middle number in the first two sets. Find the missing number and mark it on the answer sheet.

Example   (10 [30] 20)   (6 [18] 12)   (8 [?] 16)

Answer   **24**

Solution   In the first two sets, the middle number is found by adding the two other numbers in the set. Following this pattern, the missing middle number is 8 + 16 = **24**.

51   (45 [25] 20)   (36 [18] 18)   (54 [?] 18)

A 34   **B** 18   **C** 36   **D** 42   **E** 26

52   (31 [85] 23)   (16 [56] 24)   (19 [?] 56)

A 94   **B** 104   **C** 109   **D** 131   **E** 115

53   (3 [8] 24)   (4 [8] 32)   (11 [?] 55)

A 25   **B** 50   **C** 55   **D** 15   **E** 5

54   (65 [109] 44)   (7 [13] 6)   (24 [?] 32)

A 54   **B** 66   **C** 50   **D** 64   **E** 56

55   (3 [12] 9)   (4 [28] 18)   (16 [?] 31)

A 30   **B** 36   **C** 42   **D** 15   **E** 47

56   (4 [72] 9)   (2 [24] 6)   (15 [?] 5)

A 105   **B** 150   **C** 135   **D** 75   **E** 90

57   (12 [39] 9)   (10 [49] 13)   (5 [?] 14)

A 41   **B** 35   **C** 43   **D** 51   **E** 47

PLEASE GO ON TO THE NEXT PAGE

In these sentences, a word of **four letters** is hidden at the **end** of one word and the **beginning** of the next word.

Find the pair of words that contains the hidden word and mark this answer on the answer sheet.

Example   The dog was startled by the noise.

Answer   then

Solution   In this sentence, the hidden four-letter word is '**then**', which is made up of the first three letters of the word '**the**' and the first letter of the word '**n**oise'.

58 The train continued slowly for miles.

A The train **B** train continued **C** continued slowly **D** slowly for **E** for miles.

59 They hope starting ballet lessons will help her.

A They hope **B** hope starting **C** starting ballet **D** ballet lessons **E** lessons will

60 Doctors aid their patients in any way they can.

A Doctors aid **B** aid their **C** their patients **D** patients in **E** in any

61 The old device was poorly constructed.

A The old **B** old device **C** device was **D** was poorly **E** poorly constructed.

62 There was a natural order to the shapes.

A There was **B** was a **C** a natural **D** natural order **E** order to

63 The ship leaves for Barbados tomorrow.

A The ship **B** ship leaves **C** leaves for **D** for Barbados **E** Barbados tomorrow.

64 Children should never be left alone.

A Children should **B** should never **C** never be **D** be left **E** left alone.

65 It emits a strange odour when frightened.

A It emits **B** emits a **C** a strange **D** strange odour **E** odour when

PLEASE GO ON TO THE NEXT PAGE

Read the following information, then find the correct answer to the question and mark it on the answer sheet.

66
York is 25 miles from Leeds.

Leeds is 45 miles from Hull.

York is north of Hull.

Hull is directly east of Leeds.

Which of the following statements must be true?

A   York is 70 miles from Hull.

B   York is 25 miles north of Hull.

C   Leeds is south of York.

D   York is east of Hull.

E   York is west of Hull.

In these questions, there are two pairs of words. Only **one** of the five possible answers will go equally well with **both** of these pairs. Mark it on the answer sheet.

Example   (globe   planet)   (soil   mud)

Select from (pebble   earth   sand   star   dig)

Answer   **earth**

67 (month   time)   (flavour   spice)

A season   B taste   C week   D relish   E day

68 (mark   stamp)   (make   label)

A brand   B carve   C ticket   D print   E tag

69 (shrink   reduce)   (agreement   document)

A minute   B hide   C harmony   D contract   E record

70 (source   origin)   (stem   leaf)

A root   B spring   C bark   D branch   E well

71 (lock   fasten)   (flash   lightning)

A thunder   B streak   C catch   D bolt   E seal

72 (stretch   extend)   (winch   hoist)

A belt   B lift   C tackle   D reach   E crane

73 (spin   rotate)   (change   become)

A extend   B switch   C grow   D propel   E turn

PLEASE GO ON TO THE NEXT PAGE

In these sentences, the words in capitals have both had the same letter taken out. The other letters are then scrambled.

Find the letter that has been taken out of both words.

The sentence that you make must make sense.

Mark the correct three letter word on the answer sheet.

Example	I **ELI** reading **SOBO**.
Answer	K
Solution	The letter that has been removed from both words is **K**.
	The words should be **like** and **books**, as the sentence should read: I like reading books.

74 I **EAH NREE** seen anyone so incompetent.

   A S   B R   C C   D V   E P

75 I was **ELA** to deal with the **MPEROL** quite easily.

   A B   B D   C T   D I   E N

76 He was **OOGNIL** for a pair of **OCSS** to wear.

   A N   B G   C K   D P   E R

77 He **ISLE** in a quiet **LLGAIE** in the countryside.

   A D   B T   C R   D M   E V

78 You need to **RAWE** your plants **NOFE**.

   A T   B N   C F   D R   E L

79 The **KIG** wore a **ROCW** on his head.

   A C   B S   C E   D G   E N

80 A new **DMASTU** is being built near the **CYT** centre.

   A I   B R   C U   D N   E E

END OF TEST

FIRST PAST THE POST

Answers Sheets

Verbal Reasoning: Practice Papers

Multiple Choice Book 2

FIRST PAST THE POST SERIES BY ELEVENPLUSEXAMS

Pupil's Name:
School Name:
Date of Test: / /

VERBAL REASONING: TEST A

Answer like this ▬

PUPIL NUMBER
[0]	[0]	[0]	[0]	[0]
[1]	[1]	[1]	[1]	[1]
[2]	[2]	[2]	[2]	[2]
[3]	[3]	[3]	[3]	[3]
[4]	[4]	[4]	[4]	[4]
[5]	[5]	[5]	[5]	[5]
[6]	[6]	[6]	[6]	[6]
[7]	[7]	[7]	[7]	[7]
[8]	[8]	[8]	[8]	[8]
[9]	[9]	[9]	[9]	[9]

EXAM CENTRE
[0]	[0]	[0]	[0]	[0]	[0]
[1]	[1]	[1]	[1]	[1]	[1]
[2]	[2]	[2]	[2]	[2]	[2]
[3]	[3]	[3]	[3]	[3]	[3]
[4]	[4]	[4]	[4]	[4]	[4]
[5]	[5]	[5]	[5]	[5]	[5]
[6]	[6]	[6]	[6]	[6]	[6]
[7]	[7]	[7]	[7]	[7]	[7]
[8]	[8]	[8]	[8]	[8]	[8]
[9]	[9]	[9]	[9]	[9]	[9]

DATE OF BIRTH
Day	Month	Year
[0] [0]	January	2007
[1] [1]	February	2008
[2] [2]	March	2009
[3] [3]	April	2010
[4]	May	2011
[5]	June	2012
[6]	July	2013
[7]	August	2014
[8]	September	2015
[9]	October	2016
	November	2017
	December	2018

---

1 HL, IL, GL, HM, IM

2 FR, KQ, FU, JQ, KU

3 AS, BR, AT, BS, AR

4 VR, BK, PQ, DN, WP

5 MN, NN, MO, MM, NO

6 FS, TH, BN, RT, JQ

7 VE, UC, WD, VC, VD

8 stool, furniture, sit | nail, down, tool

9 ball, see, two | nostril, knows, smell

10 book, dare, study | only, whole, trap

11 transport, wheel, bush | night, bath, cricket

12 green, went, stop | does, red, did

13 clean, dry, clothes | scissors, strike, pierce

14 chimney, brick, human | snow, straw, deer

15 tar, cur, hat, car, cat

16 the, her, hat, hit, get

17 wet, low, wag, law, leg

18 hid, her, red, his, doe

19 hail, bush, bash, lush, bars

20 sing, rose, tore, wing, grow

21 coal, rock, rack, race, cold

22 25, 26, 28, 31, 33

23 board, hardy, painful, heavy, tough

24 band, cast, chuck, staff, company

25 field, hard, ring, stable, cage

26 slim, fall, lean, slender, limber

© 2019 ElevenPlusExams.co.uk — COPYING STRICTLY PROHIBITED

VERBAL REASONING: TEST A

27	28	29	30	31	32
luggage	lace	plain	S	I	L
hamper	ribbon	conduct	I	R	M
box	bow	direct	L	A	E
case	yield	explicit	T	N	R
trunk	salute	guide	C	L	H

33	34	35	36	37	38
S	W	D	Y	1	43
N	C	R	R	7	63
V	N	N	C	2	55
R	D	P	D	4	31
H	P	S	N	3	49

39	40	41	42	43
23	17	18	3	17
39	25	36	30	27
25	19	48	17	23
47	7	12	26	11
35	15	24	13	15

44	
cover	separate
merge	study
arrange	discover

45		46		47	
success	danger	object	insert	extend	satisfy
miracle	facade	investigate	approve	provoke	shorten
safety	fear	destroy	confirm	classify	lengthen

48		49		50	
enforce	force	menacing	hardy	sensitive	extraordinary
enlarge	permit	slow	weak	healthy	tender
enter	shrink	robust	ponderous	mundane	astute

51	52	53	54	55	56	57
p	h	m	p	d	p	m
t	g	d	r	k	s	g
k	e	e	b	n	a	e
g	k	t	w	t	b	d
b	m	c	d	h	d	t

58	59	60	61	62	63	64
42	41	67	31	23	3	24
39	32	55	32	20	5	18
45	36	59	33	19	6	27
41	34	68	34	21	9	30
49	49	65	35	18	8	21

VERBAL REASONING: TEST A

65
83	
78	
85	
87	
81	

66
1st	
2nd	
3rd	
4th	
5th	

67
deck		bird	
gold		fish	
ship		cat	

68
for		give	
fat		through	
fan		rest	

69
be		con	
star		cause	
hat		leave	

70
come		rest	
stand		back	
chest		slip	

71
head		knot	
stone		flow	
sea		line	

72
wind		blow	
war		let	
trap		mill	

73
white		paper	
drop		right	
sand		eye	

74
NO	
OR	
FS	
PS	
QO	

75
VY	
YC	
VC	
YF	
YC	

76
JY	
IY	
JX	
IZ	
IA	

77
QS	
RS	
QT	
QR	
RQ	

78
MQ	
QM	
QG	
QQ	
MG	

79
CD	
SP	
GH	
NH	
IQ	

80
ZW	
SG	
HH	
TG	
ZH	

BLANK PAGE

FIRST PAST THE POST SERIES BY ELEVENPLUSEXAMS

Pupil's Name

School Name

Date of Test / /

VERBAL REASONING: TEST B

Answer like this ▬

PUPIL NUMBER

EXAM CENTRE

DATE OF BIRTH

Day	Month	Year
[0]	[0] January	2007
[1]	[1] February	2008
[2]	[2] March	2009
[3]	[3] April	2010
	[4] May	2011
	[5] June	2012
	[6] July	2013
	[7] August	2014
	[8] September	2015
	[9] October	2016
	November	2017
	December	2018

---

1 A B C D E
2 A B C D E
3 A B C D E
4 A B C D E
5 A B C D E
6 A B C D E
7 A B C D E

8 g h o s t
9 s t o n e
10 p a i n t
11 h o a r d
12 b r e a c
13 h o u s e
14 s p l a h

15 CQ CP CS AQ CR
16 OV PW SV QW OW
17 FR VR FQ FP VQ
18 DP BO DN CO CP
19 DX EX MP EP DP
20 RF SF SG SE RE
21 QP QQ RP QR PQ

22 OK PK OJ PJ QK
23 A B C D E
24 It's our / our own / own brand / brand we're / we're selling.
25 No unicorns / unicorns have / have ever / ever actually / actually existed.
26 It only / only lasted / lasted for / for two / two minutes.

27 I'm asking / asking because / because we're / we're quite / quite worried.
28 The bystanders / bystanders ignored / ignored my / my pleas / pleas for
29 We called / called the / the fire / fire brigade / brigade after
30 I would / would much / much rather / rather be / be somewhere

© 2019 ElevenPlusExams.co.uk

VERBAL REASONING: TEST B

31
- 46
- 56
- 72
- 66
- 71

32
- 5
- 4
- 6
- 9
- 8

33
- 156
- 152
- 144
- 148
- 132

34
- 14
- 46
- 17
- 29
- 34

35
- 105
- 97
- 113
- 96
- 73

36
- 93
- 98
- 87
- 84
- 111

37
- 64
- 72
- 84
- 96
- 108

38
- Tuesday
- Saturday
- Friday
- Thursday
- Sunday

39
- orchid
- blue
- elm
- rose
- daisy

40
- know
- eye
- sight
- sound
- taste

41
- collect
- spend
- gather
- save
- exchange

42
- lounge
- floor
- kitchen
- bedroom
- house

43
- direct
- blunt
- round
- honest
- sharp

44
- cousin
- uncle
- grandson
- nephew
- child

45
- fast
- rapid
- speed
- brisk
- slow

46
- AZJD
- BZJD
- AZLD
- ACJD
- BZLD

47
- LICK
- LEAK
- LOCK
- LIST
- LATE

48
- JPTF
- JLTF
- IPUF
- IPTI
- JPUI

49
- PARK
- VENT
- BASK
- HEAL
- LUSH

50
- GMBU
- EKZU
- EMBS
- GKZS
- EMZU

51
- RAMP
- RICE
- POSE
- OOZE
- QUIT

52
- SECQ
- SIBS
- SEBQ
- UECQ
- UIBS

53
- greedy
- angry
- weary
- joyous
- tired
- miserable

54
- touch
- hit
- lean
- bounce
- strike
- fall

55
- throw
- transfer
- give
- spend
- carry
- place

56
- firm
- office
- branch
- produce
- stiff
- factory

57
- understand
- relief
- pursue
- chase
- believe
- explain

58
- decide
- collide
- disturb
- interrupt
- collapse
- demise

59
- mystical
- morose
- turgid
- cryptic
- multiple
- sullen

VERBAL REASONING: TEST B

60	61	62	63	64	65	66
s	h	a	g	n	m	c
b	b	n	s	r	d	g
f	l	e	b	d	w	k
h	d	o	h	h	b	z
l	s	t	t	t	t	s

67	68	69	70	71	72
b	2405	SLIP	32400	WRAP	1674
m	1046	SWAP	31044	SING	9861
e	3945	PAIL	12400	PAST	3275
d	2905	HAIL	23844	SPAN	9374
g	3944	PAWS	21044	SPAWN	3167

73	74	75	76	77	78
PARSNIP	SAT	THE	PER	MEN	LEG
AGAINST	GET	BAT	PEN	USE	PET
RANTING	MAT	HOT	AGE	BAT	MAN
WAITING	BED	SAT	ARE	SEA	MEN
WANTING	GOT	SHE	AID	EAR	BET

79	80
SHE	SIN
FOR	RIG
BET	OPT
SIT	PIN
LAB	LET

BLANK PAGE

FIRST PAST THE POST SERIES BY ELEVENPLUSEXAMS

Pupil's Name

School Name

Date of Test / /

VERBAL REASONING: TEST C

Answer like this ▬

PUPIL NUMBER

EXAM CENTRE

DATE OF BIRTH

Day	Month	Year
[0] [0]	January	2007
[1] [1]	February	2008
[2] [2]	March	2009
[3] [3]	April	2010
[4]	May	2011
[5]	June	2012
[6]	July	2013
[7]	August	2014
[8]	September	2015
[9]	October	2016
	November	2017
	December	2018

1
s
h
o
c
k

2
b
e
a
c
h

3
h
o
n
e
y

4
s
h
i
f
t

5
p
l
n
e
t

6
b
r
o
w
n

7
f
o
r
c
e

8
59
61
69
63
65

9
9
8
6
10
4

10
38
48
36
33
42

11
79
84
74
69
89

12
192
169
144
125
100

13
71
75
61
54
65

14
45
96
24
42
51

15
upload
pressure
survive
inform
perish
delete

16
emotional
gigantic
friendly
ambitious
quiet
hostile

17
gift
perpetual
absent
present
gradual
vague

18
illegal
vulgar
legendary
lawful
chaotic
neutral

19
senseless
vain
fighter
eager
modest
power

20
exotic
remote
winding
mobile
nearby
convenient

21
redundant
useless
involved
complex
complete
employed

22
Tennis
Football
Rugby
Ice hockey
Lacrosse

23
owe
let
few
lot
wet

24
lie
rid
led
kid
die

25
sham
meat
hart
stem
sear

© 2019 ElevenPlusExams.co.uk — COPYING STRICTLY PROHIBITED

VERBAL REASONING: TEST C

26	27	28	29	30	31
fast	wed	one	that	She took	Friendly people
fate	set	cat	seal	took the	people like
sick	wet	nod	seat	the day	like engaging
feat	sew	act	tint	day off	engaging in
salt	she	can	teal	off ill.	in conversations.

32	33	34	35	36
Children grow	He's older	It meant	Dogs still	A crescent
grow ashamed	older than	meant something	still impress	crescent moon
ashamed of	than he	something was	impress me	moon lit
of their	he might	was very	me when	lit up
their parents.	might look.	very wrong.	when they	up the

37	38	39	40	41	42
A	A	A	A	A	A
B	B	B	B	B	B
C	C	C	C	C	C
D	D	D	D	D	D
E	E	E	E	E	E

43	44	45	46	47	48
A	m	s	m	n	m
B	e	t	p	t	e
C	s	d	k	m	k
D	l	n	h	p	s
E	f	h	d	l	d

49	50	51	52	53	54
l	r	HART	ZBCQ	BARK	TAME
s	d	GRAB	AGCT	LEAD	GOAL
r	g	KING	WCYP	BANK	THAN
p	p	GROW	VBZQ	GOLD	FOLD
n	a	HOME	WGCT	SICK	GAME

55	56	57	58	59	60
FBSR	MKII	SOLE	right	star	damage
FCVX	NKIJ	HALT	sad	lamp	medicine
DYSS	MKIJ	TIME	left	stone	harm
FBWY	MLII	SALE	correct	candle	bandage
DEXA	NLIJ	SHOE	down	shine	injure

VERBAL REASONING: TEST C

61
- bitter
- sweet
- taste
- sour
- food

62
- flour
- salt
- mustard
- bread
- vinegar

63
- journey
- fall
- trip
- destination
- voyage

64
- season
- winter
- autumn
- cold
- spring

65
- complete
- retire
- total
- finish
- entire

66
- A
- B
- C
- D
- E

67
- meet
- savoury
- vegetable
- fruit
- sour
- melon

68
- king
- rule
- princess
- doe
- horns
- ewe

69
- round
- air
- party
- water
- carry
- sports

70
- scales
- kilogram
- flour
- water
- capacity
- metric

71
- scale
- swim
- school
- song
- robin
- flock

72
- up
- south
- compass
- sports
- within
- internal

73
- hammer
- finger
- attach
- key
- lightning
- spanner

74
- HN
- GM
- GO
- HM
- GN

75
- AQ
- CQ
- CD
- CR
- AP

76
- MK
- KL
- KN
- KK
- LK

77
- AC
- BD
- AD
- AE
- CA

78
- YL
- XL
- YM
- XA
- XM

79
- TJ
- TB
- SV
- EJ
- RV

80
- KU
- KR
- HU
- IU
- HR

FIRST PAST THE POST SERIES BY ELEVENPLUSEXAMS

Pupil's Name

School Name

Date of Test / /

VERBAL REASONING: TEST D

Answer like this ▭

1
- 26
- 17
- 28
- 13
- 23

2
- 4
- 9
- 2
- 19
- 12

3
- 16
- 18
- 23
- 11
- 15

4
- 25
- 18
- 5
- 9
- 15

5
- 36
- 6
- 46
- 26
- 16

6
- 83
- 84
- 81
- 73
- 71

7
- 8
- 3
- 18
- 15
- 11

8
- cold
- fill
- drag
- search
- on
- card

9
- must
- par
- further
- send
- more
- rat

10
- for
- pick
- under
- pocket
- tie
- shoe

11
- take
- rain
- water
- ring
- sing
- forest

12
- rat
- more
- draw
- her
- rage
- grid

13
- rain
- pea
- brow
- skill
- sing
- skin

14
- tag
- man
- bud
- park
- get
- mask

15
- LAG
- RID
- INN
- AND
- DAY

16
- RED
- BAR
- NOT
- ACT
- CON

17
- LIP
- PIN
- TAP
- ATE
- AND

18
- CAR
- MAN
- BED
- POT
- SON

19
- SET
- RAT
- SEW
- PIN
- TAG

20
- ALL
- ART
- OUT
- ARC
- USE

21
- BUT
- CON
- SIX
- PAT
- PEN

22
- RUE
- ADD
- BAT
- ANT
- TEA

23
- Romera
- Craig
- Gene
- Fatima
- Merida

VERBAL REASONING: TEST D

24		25		26	
introduce / terminate		grateful / lucky		remember / mumble	
drive / suffer		unlikely / tricky		murmur / feeble	
regret / launch		fortunate / stocky		confuse / tremble	

27		28		29	
question / consider		hardy / arrogant		loop / chain	
ponder / panic		strict / direct		string / coil	
wonder / answer		zealous / enthusiastic		stick / pin	

30		31	32	33	34
shy / muddled		w	g	h	b
fragile / curious		r	r	e	o
unusual / brave		u	a	a	u
		n	t	r	n
		g	e	t	d

35	36	37	38	39	40
h	c	s	7362	BANJO	82754
o	h	h	8370	BATON	52689
i	a	o	5285	SETUP	12705
s	r	v	1954	BEANS	81270
t	t	e	6284	PLEAT	56982

41	42	43	44	45	46
9351	SPEAR	9537	snow	cold	ban
1539	SPIRE	3519	know	sold	nob
9531	PASTE	9413	stow	cods	cab
3753	PINES	4873	sow	clod	cob
3486	TRAIN	5397	now	olds	nab

47	48	49	50	51	52
meal	raw	war	lame	34	94
tame	was	and	male	18	104
late	sad	raw	pale	36	109
teal	war	wan	plea	42	131
mate	saw	awn	meal	26	115

53	54	55	56	57	58
25	54	30	105	41	The train
50	66	36	150	35	train continued
55	50	42	135	43	continued slowly
15	64	15	75	51	slowly for
5	56	47	90	47	for miles.

VERBAL REASONING: TEST D

59	60	61	62
They hope	Doctors aid	The old	There was
hope starting	aid their	old device	was a
starting ballet	their patients	device was	a natural
ballet lessons	patients in	was poorly	natural order
lessons will	in any	poorly constructed.	order to

63	64	65	66
The ship	Children should	It emits	A
ship leaves	should never	emits a	B
leaves for	never be	a strange	C
for Barbados	be left	strange odour	D
Barbadoro tomorrow.	left alone.	odour when	E

67	68	69	70	71	72
season	brand	minute	root	thunder	belt
taste	carve	hide	spring	streak	lift
week	ticket	harmony	bark	catch	tackle
relish	print	contract	branch	bolt	reach
day	tag	record	well	seal	crane

73	74	75	76	77	78
extend	S	B	N	D	T
switch	R	D	G	T	N
grow	C	T	K	R	F
propel	V	I	P	M	R
turn	P	N	R	V	L

79	80
C	I
S	R
E	U
G	N
N	E

FIRST PAST THE POST

Answers & Explanations

Verbal Reasoning: Practice Papers

Multiple Choice

Book 2

VERBAL REASONING: TEST A

Question	Answer	Explanation
1	HL	The letter series follows the pattern of + 1 for the first letter in the pair and + 1 for the second letter in the pair, i.e., G + 1 = **H**, and K + 1 = **L**.
2	JQ	The letter series follows the pattern of + 2 for the first letter in the pair and - 2 for the second letter in the pair, i.e., H + 2 = **J**, and S - 2 = **Q**.
3	AR	The letter series follows the pattern of - 3 for the first letter in the pair and - 3 for the second letter in the pair, i.e., D - 3 = **A**, and U - 3 = **R**.
4	VR	The letter series follows the pattern of + 1 for the first letter in the pair and + 2 for the second letter in the pair, i.e., U + 1 = **V**, and P + 2 = **R**.
5	MN	The letter series follows the pattern of + 1, + 2, + 3... for the first letter in the pair and - 1. - 2, - 3... for the second letter in the pair, i.e., I + 4 = **M**, and R - 4 = **N**.
6	FS	The letter series follows the pattern of - 4 for the first letter in the pair and + 3 for the second letter in the pair, i.e., J - 4 = **F**, and P + 3 = **S**.
7	VD	The letter series follows the pattern of -5 for the first letter in the pair and + 1, + 3, + 5, + 7... for the second letter in the pair, i.e., A - 5 = **V**, and W + 7 = **D**.
8	**furniture** and **tool**	Both '**furniture** and '**tool**' are categories. A 'chair' is a type of furniture and a 'hammer' is a type of 'tool'.
9	**see** and **smell**	Both '**see**' and '**smell**' are functions. The 'eye' is used to 'see', and the 'nose' is used to 'smell'.
10	**dare** and **trap**	Both '**dare**' and '**trap**' are anagrams. 'Dare' is an anagram of 'read', and 'trap' is an anagram of 'part'.
11	**bush** and **bath**	Both '**bush**' and '**bath**' are the original word with a H added. 'Bus' becomes 'bush' and 'bat' becomes 'bath'.
12	**went** and **did**	Both '**went**' and '**did**' are in the past tense. 'Went' is the past tense of 'go' and 'did' is the past tense of 'do'.
13	**clean** and **pierce**	Both '**clean**' and '**pierce**' are synonyms. 'Clean' is a synonym of 'wash' and 'piece' is a synonym of 'cut'.
14	**brick** and **snow**	Both '**brick**' and '**snow**' are components. 'Brick' is a component of a 'house' and 'snow' is a component of an 'igloo'.
15	car	From the first word, use the 3rd letter (**c**). From the second word, use the 1st letter (**a**). From the first word, use the 2nd letter (**r**).
16	her	From the second word, use the 1st letter (**h**). From the first word, use the 1st and 3rd letters (**e, r**).
17	law	From the second word use the 5th and 4th letters (**l, a**). From the first word use the 5th letter (**w**).
18	hid	From the first word, use the 1st and 2nd letters (**h, i**). From the second word, use the 6th letter (**d**).
19	lush	From the first word, use the 4th letter (**l**). From the second word, use the 2nd, 3rd and 4th letters (**u, s, h**).
20	sing	From the first word, use the 5th letter (**s**). From the second word, use the 2nd and 3rd letters (**i, n**). From the first word, use the 2nd letter (**g**).
21	cold	From the first word, use the 2nd letter (**c**). From the second word, use the 2nd and 1st letter (**o, l**). From the first word, use the 6th letter (**d**).

VERBAL REASONING: TEST A

Question	Answer	Explanation
22	31	Georgina is **18** years old. Rocco is 5 years older than Georgina, so he is **23** years old. Anita is a year older than Rocco, so she is **24** years old. Ben is a year older than Anita, so he is **25** years old. Eva is 6 years older than Ben, so she is **31**. **Therefore, the answer is 31.**
23	tough	The word '**tough**' can describe something that is hard in difficulty or it can describe something that is physically strong. The word goes equally well with 'rigid' / 'stiff' and 'difficult' / 'strenuous'.
24	cast	The word '**cast**' can describe the group of actors featuring in a film/play/musical or can describe the action of throwing something out. The word goes equally well with 'throw' / 'hurl' and 'performers' / 'actors'.
25	stable	The word '**stable**' can describe the place where a horse is kept or it can describe something as physically secure. The word goes equally well with 'pen' / 'enclosure' and 'firm' / 'sturdy'.
26	lean	The word '**lean**' can describe the angle in which something is or it can describe the weight/physicality of a person. The word goes equally well with 'tilt' / 'slope' and 'thin' / 'haggard'.
27	trunk	The word '**trunk**' can describe the body of a person or it can describe a box to keep items in. The word goes equally well with 'body' / 'torso' and 'chest' / 'crate'.
28	bow	The word '**bow**' can describe a polite way to greet royalty or those superior to you or it can describe the outcome of tying a piece of long fabric. The word goes equally well with 'curtsy' / 'nod' and 'loop' / 'knot'.
29	direct	The word '**direct**' can describe a commanding action or it can describe the way in which someone talks - forthright. The word goes equally well with 'lead' / 'manage' and 'frank' / 'honest'.
30	L	The missing letter is '**L**'. THGSEN becomes '**length**' and OPO becomes '**pool**'.
31	N	The missing letter is '**N**'. CEHGSA becomes '**changes**' and IMD becomes '**mind**'.
32	R	The missing letter is '**R**'. PYADE becomes '**prayed**' and USLTSE becomes '**results**'.
33	H	The missing letter is '**H**'. OELW becomes '**whole**' and ITW becomes '**with**'.
34	W	The missing letter is '**W**'. SRFELO becomes '**flowers**' and GOR becomes '**grow**'.
35	D	The missing letter is '**D**'. IRVE becomes '**drive**' and SIE becomes '**side**'.
36	Y	The missing letter is '**Y**'. EONM becomes '**money**' and UB becomes '**buy**'.
37	1	If you substitute ? = 1, then you reach the solution: 4 x 3 ÷ 2 = 28 ÷ 4 - **1** (both sides equal 6).
38	31	If you substitute ? = 31, then you reach the solution: 17 x 4 = 9 x 11 - **31** (both sides equal 68).
39	35	If you substitute ? = 35, then you reach the solution: 53 + 72 - 36 = 6 x 9 + **35** (both sides equal 89).
40	25	If you substitute ? = 25, then you reach the solution: 72 ÷ 4 - 3 = 80 ÷ 2 - **25** (both sides equal 15).
41	18	If you substitute ? = 18, then you reach the solution: 66 ÷ 11 x 6 = 3 x 6 + **18** (both sides equal 36).
42	13	If you substitute ? = 13, then you reach the solution: 63 ÷ 3 + 29 = 7 x 9 - **13** (both sides equal 50).
43	17	If you substitute ? = 17, then you reach the solution: 12 x 4 - 7 = 72 ÷ 3 + **17** (both sides equal 41).
44	**merge** and **separate**	The two words most opposite in meaning are '**merge**' and '**separate**'. 'Merge' means to combine two or more things, whereas 'separate' means to move two or more things apart.

VERBAL REASONING: TEST A

Question	Answer	Explanation
45	**safety** and **danger**	The words most opposite in meaning are '**safety**' and '**danger**'. 'Safety' means to be away from danger, whereas 'danger' mean to be in harm's way.
46	**object** and **approve**	The words most opposite in meaning are '**object**' and '**approve**'. 'Object' means to oppose something, whereas 'approve' means to agree with something.
47	**extend** and **shorten**	The words most opposite in meaning are '**extend**' and '**shorten**'. 'Extend' means to increase the length of something, whereas 'shorten' means to decrease the length of something.
48	**enlarge** and **shrink**	The words most opposite in meaning are '**enlarge**' and '**shrink**'. 'Enlarge' means to make something bigger, whereas 'shrink' means to make something smaller.
49	**robust** and **weak**	The words most opposite in meaning are '**robust**' and '**weak**'. 'Robust' means strong and durable, whereas 'weak' means frail and lacking strength.
50	**mundane** and **extraordinary**	The words most opposite in meaning are '**mundane**' and '**extraordinary**'. 'Mundane' means boring and ordinary, whereas 'extraordinary' means unusual and astounding.
51	g	The letter '**g**' completes the four words: stin**g**, **g**ate, ho**g**, **g**rave.
52	k	The letter '**k**' completes the four words: pec**k**, **k**it, thin**k**, **k**iss.
53	d	The letter '**d**' completes the four words: wil**d**, **d**ark, lou**d**, **d**esk.
54	w	The letter '**w**' completes the four words: kne**w**, **w**ide, stra**w**, **w**ake.
55	t	The letter '**t**' completes the four words: hoo**t**, **t**our, whe**t**, **t**ilt.
56	a	The letter '**a**' completes the four words: **a**rena, **a**id, ple**a**, **a**unt.
57	g	The letter '**g**' completes the four words: bra**g**, **g**ust, brin**g**, **g**houl.
58	41	In this sequence, each term is given by adding 6 to the previous term. Therefore, the next term is 35 + 6 = **41**.
59	36	This is a sequence of consecutive, ascending square numbers. Therefore, the next term is 6^2 = **36**.
60	55	In this sequence, each term is given by a repeating pattern of - 5, + 8, -5, + 8, etc. Therefore, the next term is 60 - 5 = **55**.
61	33	In this sequence, each term is given by an increasing pattern of + 1, + 2, + 3, + 4, etc. Therefore, the next term is 28 + 5 = **33**.
62	20	This is a series of alternate sequences. Between odd terms, subtract by 1. Between even terms, add by 1. Therefore, the next term is 21 - 1 = **20**.
63	5	In this sequence, each term is given by a decreasing pattern of - 3, - 4, - 5, - 6, etc. Therefore, the next term is 11 - 6 = **5**.
64	30	In this sequence, each term is given by a repeating pattern of x 2, - 3, x 2. - 3, etc. Therefore, the next term is 15 x 2 = **30**.
65	81	In this sequence, each term is given by a repeating pattern of - 8, + 5, + 9, - 8, + 5, + 9, etc. Therefore, the next term is 76 + 5 = **81**.

VERBAL REASONING: TEST A

Question	Answer	Explanation
66	3rd	Lewis moves up 2 places which means he is now in 4th place (6 -2 = 4). Fernando overtook Lewis; therefore, he is in 4th place himself. He then overtakes someone else, which means he is now a place higher—**3rd place**.
67	**gold** and **fish**	'Goldfish' can be made from '**gold**' and '**fish**'.
68	**for** and **give**	'Forgive' can be made from '**for**' and '**give**'.
69	**be** and **cause**	'Because' can be made from '**be**' and '**cause**'.
70	**come** and **back**	'Comeback' can be made from '**come**' and '**back**'.
71	**head** and **line**	'Headline' can be made from '**head**' and '**line**'.
72	**wind** and **mill**	'Windmill' can be made from '**wind**' and '**mill**'.
73	**sand** and **paper**	'Sandpaper' can be made from '**sand**' and '**paper**'.
74	FS	Move + 1 for the first letter in the pair and + 1 for the second letter in the pair, i.e., E + 1 = **F**, and R + 1 = **S**.
75	VC	Move - 1 for the first letter in the pair and - 1 for the second letter in the pair, i.e., X - 2 = **V**, and E - 2 = **C**.
76	JX	Move + 4 for the first letter in the pair and + 1 for the second letter in the pair, i.e., F + 4 = **J**, and W + 1 = **X**.
77	QR	Move + 1 for the first letter in the pair and - 1 for the second letter in the pair, i.e., P + 1 = **Q**, and S - 1 = **R**.
78	QG	Move + 2 for the first letter in the pair and - 5 for the second letter in the pair, i.e., O + 2 = **Q**, and L - 5 = **G**.
79	IQ	Involves mirror letter pairs (e.g. A|Z, B|Y, C|X, etc). R mirrors **I**, and J mirrors **Q**.
80	TG	Move - 7 for the first letter in the pair and + 3 for the second letter in the pair, i.e., A - 7 = **T**, and D + 3 = **G**.

VERBAL REASONING: TEST B

Question	Answer	Explanation
1	D	3 + 9 + 3 + 6 = 21, **D** = 21
2	D	2 x 15 - 18 + 3 = 15, **D** = 15
3	E	4 x 12 ÷ 6 + 4 = 12, **E** = 12
4	B	4 x 5 - 15 - 1 = 4, **B** = 4
5	E	2 X 14 + 12 - 20 = 20, **E** = 20
6	C	18 ÷ (3 ÷ 2) + 2 = 14, **C** = 14
7	E	5 x 15 - 30 - 15 = 30, E = **30**
8	g	Move the letter 'g' to make 'host' and 'thin**g**'.
9	s	Move the letter 's' to make 'tone' and 'hat**s**'.
10	t	Move the letter 't' to make 'pain' and '**t**hose'.
11	o	Move the letter 'o' to make 'hard' and '**o**range'.
12	r	Move the letter 'r' to make 'beach' and 'w**r**ing'.
13	u	Move the letter 'u' to make 'hose' and 'val**u**e'.
14	p	Move the letter 'p' to make 'slash' and '**p**rice'.
15	CQ	The letter series follows the pattern of + 1 for the first letter in the pair and - 1 for the second letter in the pair, i.e., B + 1 = **C**, and R - 1 = **Q**.
16	OW	The letter series follows the pattern of - 4 for the first letter in the pair and + 3 for the second letter in the pair, i.e., S - 4 = **O**, and T + 3 = **W.**
17	VQ	The letter series follows the pattern of + 1 for the first letter in the pair and - 2 for the second letter in the pair, i.e., U + 1 = **V**, and S - 2 = **Q**.
18	CO	The letter series follows the pattern of + 6 for the first letter in the pair and + 6 for the second letter in the pair, i.e., W + 6 = **C**, and I + 6 = **O**.
19	EX	The letter series follows the pattern of - 5 for the first letter in the pair and + 3 for the second letter in the pair, i.e., J - 5 = **E**, and U + 3 = **X**.
20	SE	The letter series follows the pattern of + 5 for the first letter in the pair and + 3 for the second letter in the pair, i.e., N + 5 = **S**, and B + 3 = **E**.
21	PQ	The letter series follows the pattern of - 7 for the first letter in the pair and - 7 for the second letter in the pair, i.e., W - 7 = **P**, and X - 7 = **Q**.
22	OJ	The letter series follows the pattern of - 3, - 5, - 3, - 5... for the first letter in the pair and + 4 for the second letter in the pair, i.e., T - 5 = **O**, and F + 4 = **J**.

VERBAL REASONING: TEST B

Question	Answer	Explanation
23	A	The text states that all politicians are crooks and that all crooks are liars; therefore, all politicians are liars. However, it does not say that all crooks and liars are politicians nor does it talk about the quantity of them. Therefore, the answer has to be **A**.
24	It's our	The hidden four-letter word is 'sour' (It**S OUR**).
25	No unicorns	The hidden four-letter word is 'noun' (**NO UN**icorns).
26	for two	The hidden four-letter word is 'fort' (**FOR T**wo).
27	I'm asking	The hidden four-letter word is 'mask' (I**M ASK**ing).
28	bystanders ignored	The hidden four-letter word is 'sign' (bystander**S IGN**ored).
29	brigade after	The hidden four-letter word is 'deaf' (briga**DE AF**ter).
30	rather be	The hidden four-letter word is 'herb' (rat**HER B**e).
31	66	Looking at each set as (a [b] c), then b = a + c, so the answer is 37 + 29 = **66**.
32	9	Looking at each set as (a [b] c), then b = a ÷ c, so the answer is 45 ÷ 5 = **9**.
33	156	Looking at each set as (a [b] c), then b = a x c, so the answer is 13 x 12 = **156**.
34	34	Looking at each set as (a [b] c), then b = 2(c-a), so the answer is 2(56-39) = **34**.
35	97	Looking at each set as (a [b] c), then b = ac + 1, so the answer is 6 x 16 + 1 = **97**.
36	93	Looking at each set as (a [b] c), then b = c + a ÷ 2, so the answer is 75 + 36 ÷ 2 = **93**.
37	108	Looking at each set as (a [b] c), then b = 2a + c, so the answer is 2 x 12 + 84 = **108**.
38	Friday	The current day is Monday because the day before Wednesday is Tuesday (which is tomorrow); therefore, it was Friday 3 days ago.
39	**blue** and **elm**	The three related words are all types of flowers. Therefore, the two unconnected words are '**blue**' and '**elm**'.
40	**know** and **eye**	The three related words are all senses. Therefore, the two unconnected words are '**know**' and '**eye**'.
41	**spend** and **exchange**	The three related words are all synonyms for 'collect'. Therefore, the two unconnected words are '**spend**' and '**exchange**'.
42	**floor** and **house**	The three related words are all rooms. Therefore, the two unconnected words are '**floor**' and '**house**'.
43	**round** and **sharp**	The three related words are all synonyms for 'honest' and 'direct'. Therefore, the two unconnected words are '**round**' and '**sharp**'.
44	**cousin** and **child**	The three related words are all male relatives. Therefore, the two unconnected words are '**cousin**' and '**child**'.

VERBAL REASONING: TEST B

Question	Answer	Explanation
45	**speed** and **slow**	The three related words are all synonyms for 'fast' and 'brisk'. Therefore, the two unconnected words are '**speed**' and '**slow**'.
46	BZJD	The word 'GULL' is coded as 'FTKK'. Each letter has changed according to the following rule: - 1. - 1, - 1,- 1. Therefore, 'CAKE' is coded as '**BZJD**'.
47	LICK	The word 'LIST' is coded as 'NKUV'. Each letter has changed according to the following rule: + 2, + 2, + 2, + 2. The inverse of this rule is - 2, - 2, - 2, - 2. Therefore, the code 'NKEM' generated the word '**LICK**'.
48	JLTF	The word 'YELL' is coded as 'CHNM'. Each letter has changed according to the following rule: + 4, + 3, + 2, + 1. Therefore, 'FIRE' is coded as **JLTF**.
49	HEAL	The word 'BLOT' is coded as 'YOLG'. Each letter has changed into its corresponding mirror letter partner. Therefore, the code 'SVZO' generated the word '**HEAL**'.
50	EMZU	The word 'ROPE' is coded as 'QPOF'. Each letter has changed according to the following rule: -1, +1, -1, +1. Therefore, 'FLAT' is coded as '**EMZU**'.
51	OOZE	The word 'CUFF' is coded as 'DRAB'. Each letter has changed according to the following rule: + 1, - 3, - 5, - 4. The inverse of this rule is - 1. + 3. + 5, + 4. Therefore, the code 'PLUA' generated the word '**OOZE**'.
52	UECQ	The word 'COMB' is coded as 'DLOY'. Each letter has changed according to the following rule: + 1, - 3, + 2, - 3. Therefore, 'THAT' is coded as '**UECQ**'.
53	**weary** and **tired**	The two words closest in meaning are '**weary**' and '**tired**'. Both words are synonyms for 'sleepy' and 'exhausted'.
54	**hit** and **strike**	The words closest in meaning are '**hit**' and '**strike**'. Both words are synonyms for 'attack' and 'afflict'.
55	**transfer** and **carry**	The words closest in meaning are '**transfer**' and '**carry**'. Both words are synonyms for 'move' and 'shift'.
56	**firm** and **stiff**	The words closest in meaning are '**firm**' and '**stiff**'. Both words are synonyms for 'rigid' and 'hard'.
57	**pursue** and **chase**	The words closest in meaning are '**pursue**' and '**chase**'. Both words are synonyms for 'follow' and 'track'.
58	**disturb** and **interrupt**	The words closest in meaning are '**disturb**' and '**interrupt**'. Both words are synonyms for 'distract' and 'bother'.
59	**morose** and **sullen**	The words closest in meaning are '**morose**' and '**sullen**'. Both words are synonyms for 'miserable' and 'glum'.

VERBAL REASONING: TEST B

Question	Answer	Explanation
60	h	The letter 'h' completes the four words: too**h**, **h**ind, mas**h**, **h**ead.
61	s	The letter 's' completes the four words: pas**s**, **s**oup, her**s**, **s**eek.
62	e	The letter 'e' completes the four words: sal**e**, **e**nd, bar**e**, **e**yes.
63	g	The letter 'g' completes the four words: bu**g**, **g**rid, sin**g**, **g**as.
64	n	The letter 'n' completes the four words: see**n**, **n**est, whe**n**, **n**ose.
65	t	The letter 't' completes the four words: sli**t**, **t**ail, pan**t**, **t**alk.
66	k	'The letter 'k' completes the four words: sul**k**, **k**iln, ris**k**, **k**not.
67	m	The letter 'm' completes the four words: bri**m**, **m**aid, drea**m**, **m**ore.
68	2405	0 = A, 1 = H, 2 = S, 3 = W, 4 = L, 5 = P, 6 = T, and 9 = I SLAP PASS WILL HALT 2405 5022 3944 1046 Therefore, the correct code for 'SLAP' is **2405.**
69	PAWS	The word with the code 5032 is '**PAWS**' *(see code in 68 above)*.
70	21044	The correct code for 'SHALL' is **21044** *(see code in 68 above)*.
71	WRAP	1 = P, 2 = I, 3 = S, 4 = T, 5 = G, 6 = A, 7 = N, 8 = R, and 9 = W SING WRAP SPAN PANT 3275 9861 3167 1674 Therefore, the correct word with the code 9861 is '**WRAP**'.
72	3167	The correct code for 'SPAN' is **3167** *(see code in 71 above)*.
73	RANTING	The word with the code '8674275' is '**RANTING**' *(see code in 71 above)*.
74	GET	The missing three-letter word from 'FOR**GET**' is '**GET**'.
75	SAT	The missing three-letter word from 'CONVER**SAT**ION' is '**SAT**'.
76	AGE	The missing three-letter word from 'DAM**AGE**D' is '**AGE**'.
77	USE	The missing three-letter word from 'TRO**USE**RS' is '**USE**'.
78	LEG	The missing three-letter word from 'E**LEG**ANT' is '**LEG**'.
79	BET	The missing three-letter word from '**BET**WEEN' is '**BET**'.
80	RIG	The missing three-letter word from 'O**RIG**INALLY' is '**RIG**'.

VERBAL REASONING: TEST C

Question	Answer	Explanation
1	h	Move the letter 'h' to make 'sock' and 'maths'.
2	b	Move the letter 'b' to make 'each' and 'bread'.
3	y	Move the letter 'y' to make 'hone' and 'yearn'.
4	h	Move the letter 'h' to make 'sift' and 'tooth'.
5	e	Move the letter 'e' to make 'plant' and 'every'.
6	n	Move the letter 'n' to make 'brow' and 'snake'.
7	c	Move the letter 'c' to make 'fore' and 'crest'.
8	63	In this sequence, each term is given by adding 7 to the previous term. Therefore, the next term is 56 + 7 = **63.**
9	10	In this sequence, each term is given by a repeating pattern of - 2, - 4, - 2, - 4, etc. Therefore, the next term is 12 - 2 = **10**.
10	48	In this sequence, each term is given by an increasing pattern of + 1, + 2, + 4, + 8, + 16, etc. Therefore, the next term is 32 + 16 = **48**.
11	79	In this sequence, each term is given by a repeating pattern of + 6, + 16, + 6, + 16, etc. Therefore, the next term is 63 + 6 = **79**.
12	125	This is a sequence of consecutive, ascending cube numbers. Therefore, the next term is 5^3 = **125**.
13	71	This sequence is an example of the Fibonacci Series, a series in which terms are given by adding the two previous terms together (e.g., 1, 1, 2, 3, 5, 8). Therefore, the next term is 27 + 44 = **71**.
14	24	This is a series of alternate sequences. Between odd terms, add by 3. Between even terms, multiply by 2. Therefore, the next term is 21 + 3 = **24.**
15	**survive** and **perish**	The two words most opposite in meaning are '**survive**' and '**perish**'. 'Survive' means to stay alive, whereas 'perish' means to die.
16	**friendly** and **hostile**	The two words most opposite in meaning are '**friendly**' and '**hostile**'. 'Friendly' means kind and approachable, whereas 'hostile' means aggressive.
17	**absent** and **present**	The two words most opposite in meaning are '**absent**' and '**present**'. 'Absent' means you are not at a place/event, whereas present means you are there.
18	**illegal** and **lawful**	The two words most opposite in meaning are '**illegal**' and '**lawful**'. 'Illegal' means you do not abide by the law, whereas 'lawful' means you abide the law.
19	**vain** and **modest**	The two words most opposite in meaning are '**vain**' and '**modest**'. 'Vain' means conceited and self-centred, whereas 'modest' means humble.
20	**remote** and **nearby**	The two words most opposite in meaning are '**remote**' and '**nearby**'. 'Remote' means far away, whereas 'nearby' means close.
21	**redundant** and **employed**	The words most opposite in meaning are '**redundant**' and '**employed**'. 'Redundant' means unemployed due to lack of work, whereas 'employed' means you are hired and working.
22	Lacrosse	Tennis classes go on for 5 months. Football classes are offered for 7 months. Rugby is offered for a total of 5 months. Ice Hockey is offered for a total of 6 months. Lacrosse is offered for a total of 3 months. Therefore, the answer is **Lacrosse**.
23	wet	From the second word, use the 3rd letter (**w**). From the first word, use the 3rd letter (**e**). From the second word, use the 1st letter (**t**).

VERBAL REASONING: TEST C

Question	Answer	Explanation
24	kid	From the second word, use the 2nd letter (**k**). From the second word, use the 3rd letter (**i**). From the first word, use the 1st letter (**d**).
25	stem	From the first word, use the 1st letter (**s**). From the first word, use the 2nd letter (**t**). From the second word, use the 3rd letter (**e**). From the second word, use the 4th letter (**m**).
26	feat	From the second word, use the 1st letter (**f**). From the first word, use the 3rd letter (**e**). From the first word, use the 4th letter (**a**). From the first worse use the 2nd letter (**t**).
27	set	From the first word, use the 3rd letter (**s**). From the second word, use the 5th letter (**e**). From the first word, use the 4th letter (**t**).
28	can	From the first word, use the 1st letter (**c**). From the second word, use the 1st letter (**a**). From the second word, use the 6th letter (**n**).
29	that	From the first word, use the 3rd letter (**t**). From the second word, use the 6th letter (**h**). From the second word use the 2nd letter (**a**). From the first word, use the 3rd letter (**t**).
30	off ill	The hidden four-letter word is 'fill' (of**F ILL**).
31	like engaging	The hidden four-letter word is 'keen' (li**KE EN**gaging).
32	grow ashamed	The hidden four-letter word is 'wash' (gro**W ASH**amed).
33	He's older	The hidden four-letter word is 'sold' (He**'S OLD**er).
34	meant something	The hidden four-letter word is 'ants' (me**ANT S**omething).
35	still impress	The hidden four-letter word is 'limp' (sti**L IMP**ress).
36	A crescent	The hidden four-letter word is 'acre' (**A CRE**scent).
37	C	9 ÷ 3 + 12 - 6 = 9, **C = 9**
38	A	72 ÷ 3 ÷ 8 = 3, **A = 3**
39	D	11 x 12 ÷ 6 - 11 = 11, **D = 11**
40	E	63 ÷ 7 X 4 + 27 = 63, **E = 63**
41	D	4 x 5 + 8 - 18 = 10, **D = 10**
42	E	30 ÷ 3 + 24 - 4 = 30, **E = 30**
43	B	2 X 5 X 3 - 27 = 3, **B = 3**
44	s	The letter 's' completes the four words: glas**s**, **s**oul, fur**s**, **s**elf.
45	n	The letter 'n' completes the four words: show**n**, **n**ewt, whe**n**, **n**igh.
46	p	The letter 'p' completes the four words: cam**p**, **p**ost, sho**p**, **p**ull.
47	m	The letter 'm' completes the four words: gu**m**, **m**ilk, swa**m**, **m**ain.
48	d	The letter 'd' completes the four words: win**d**, **d**uel, bon**d**, **d**ent.
49	r	The letter 'r' completes the four words: sou**r**, **r**asp, pai**r**, **r**aid.

VERBAL REASONING: TEST C

Question	Answer	Explanation
50	a	The letter 'a' completes the four words: te**a**, **a**im, dram**a**, **a**rid.
51	GRAB	The word 'COIN' is coded as 'EQKP'. Each letter has changed according to the following rule: + 2, + 2, + 2, + 2. The inverse of this rule is - 2, - 2, - 2, - 2. Therefore, the code 'ITCD' generated the word '**GRAB**'.
52	WCYP	The word 'DEAL' is coded as 'BCYJ'. Each letter has changed according to the following rule: - 2. - 2, - 2,- 2. Therefore, 'YEAR' is coded as '**WCYP**'.
53	GOLD	The word 'FAKE' is coded as 'UZPV'. Each letter has changed into its corresponding mirror letter partner. Therefore, the code 'TLOW' generated the word '**GOLD**'.
54	GAME	The word 'SEAL' is coded as 'OCWJ'. Each letter has changed according to the following rule: - 4, - 2, - 4, - 2. The inverse of this rule is + 4, + 2, + 4, + 2. Therefore, the code 'CYIC' generated the word '**GAME**'.
55	FCVX	The word 'STAR' is coded as 'TVDV'. Each letter has changed according to the following rule: + 1, + 2, + 3, + 4. Therefore, 'EAST' is coded as '**FCVX**'.
56	MKII	The word 'OVER' is coded as 'PXHV'. Each letter has changed according to the following rule: + 1, + 2, + 3, + 4. Therefore, 'LIFE' is coded as '**MKII**'.
57	SALE	The word 'RASP' is coded as 'MYNR'. Each letter has changed according to the following rule: - 5, - 2. - 5, + 2. The inverse of this rule is + 5, + 2, + 5, - 2. Therefore, the code 'NYGG' generated the word '**SALE**'.
58	**sad** and **correct**	The three related words are all directions. Therefore, the two unconnected words are '**sad**' and '**correct**'.
59	**stone** and **shine**	The three related words are all sources of light. Therefore, the two unconnected words are '**stone**' and '**shine**'.
60	**medicine** and **bandage**	The three related words are all synonyms for mistreat. Therefore, the two unconnected words are '**medicine**' and '**bandage**'.
61	**taste** and **food**	The three related words are tastes. Therefore, the two unconnected words are '**taste**' and '**food**'.
62	**flour** and **bread**	The three related words are condiments. Therefore, the two unconnected words are '**flour**' and '**bread**'.
63	**fall** and **destination**	The three related words are synonyms for trip. Therefore, the two unconnected words are '**fall**' and '**destination**'.
64	**season** and **cold**	The three related words are seasons. Therefore, the two unconnected words are '**season**' and '**cold**'.
65	**retire** and **finish**	The three related words are synonyms for a whole. Therefore, the two unconnected words are '**retire**' and '**finish**'.

VERBAL REASONING: TEST C

Question	Answer	Explanation
66	B	Citrus fruits include oranges and lemons; therefore, it is not certain that an even number has been bought. The total of fruits bought is not mentioned. Beth could not have bought more oranges, because there are more lemons in a bag and she bought an equal number of bags. Beth's preference of fruit is never mentioned. **Which means the answer is B, because there are more lemons in a bag than oranges.**
67	**savoury** and **sour**	Both '**savoury**' and '**sour**' are tastes. The taste of 'meat' is 'savoury', and the taste of a 'lemon' is 'sour'.
68	**princess** and **ewe**	Both '**princess**' and '**ewe**' are female equivalents. A 'princess' is the female equivalent of a 'prince', and a 'ewe' is the female equivalent of a 'ram'.
69	**air** and **water**	Both '**air**' and '**water**' are the contents of a 'balloon' and a 'bottle'.
70	**flour** and **water**	Both '**flour**' and '**water**' are measured items. 'Flour' is measured in 'grams' and 'water' is measured in 'litres'.
71	**school** and **flock**	Both '**school**' and '**flock**' are collective nouns. 'School' is the collective noun for a group of 'fish', and 'flock' is the collective noun for a group of 'birds'.
72	**south** and **within**	Both '**south**' and '**within**' are antonyms. 'South' is an antonym for 'north', and 'within' is an antonym for 'outside'.
73	**hammer** and **spanner**	Both '**hammer**' and '**spanner**' are tools. A 'hammer' is the tool needed for a nail, and a 'spanner' is the tool needed to tighten a bolt.
74	GN	Move + 2 for the first letter in the pair and + 1 for the second letter in the pair, i.e., E + 2 = **G**, and M + 1 = **N**.
75	AP	Move - 1 for the first letter in the pair and - 1 for the second letter in the pair, i.e., B - 1 = **A**, and Q - 1 = **P**.
76	KK	Move + 2 for the first letter in the pair and + 2 for the second letter in the pair, i.e., I + 2 = **K**, and I + 2 = **K**.
77	AD	Move + 1 for the first letter in the pair and - 3 for the second letter in the pair, i.e., Z + 1 = **A**, and G - 3 = **D**.
78	XA	Move + 3 for the first letter in the pair and - 5 for the second letter in the pair, i.e., U + 3 = **X**, and F - 5 = **A**.
79	RV	Move + 4 for the first letter in the pair and + 5 for the second letter in the pair, i.e., N + 4 = **R**, and Q + 5 = **V**.
80	KU	Move + 7 for the first letter in the pair and + 3 for the second letter in the pair, i.e., D + 7 = **K**, and R + 3 = **U**.

VERBAL REASONING: TEST D

Question	Answer	Explanation
1	26	If you substitute ? = 26, then you reach the solution: 13 x 4 x 3 = 3 x 2 x **26** (both sides equal 156).
2	4	If you substitute ? = 4, then you reach the solution: 81 ÷ 27 + 15 = 17 + 5 - **4** (both sides equal 18).
3	18	If you substitute ? = 18, then you reach the solution: 24 + 23 - 35 = 5 x 6 - **18** (both sides equal 12).
4	5	If you substitute ? = 5, then you reach the solution: 8 x 3 + 36 = 13 x 5 - **5** (both sides equal 60).
5	16	If you substitute ? = 16, then you reach the solution: 15 x 7 - 25 = 8 x 8 + **16** (both sides equal 80).
6	83	If you substitute ? = 83, then you reach the solution: 13 x 12 - 99 = 14 x 10 - **83** (both sides equal 57).
7	3	If you substitute ? = 3, then you reach the solution: 75 - 17 - 19 = 6 x 7 - **3** (both sides equal 39).
8	**drag** and **on**	'Dragon' can be made from '**drag**' and '**on**'.
9	**further** and **more**	'Furthermore' can be made from '**further**' and '**more**'.
10	**pick** and **pocket**	'Pickpocket' can be made from '**pick**' and '**pocket**'.
11	**rain** and **forest**	'Rainforest' can be made from '**rain**' and '**forest**'.
12	**rat** and **her**	'Rather' can be made from '**rat**' and '**her**'.
13	**brow** and **sing**	'Browsing' can be made from '**brow**' and '**sing**'.
14	**bud** and **get**	'Budget' can be made from '**bud**' and '**get**'.
15	RID	The missing three-letter word from 'F**RID**AY' is '**RID**'.
16	BAR	The missing three-letter word from '**BAR**EFOOT' is '**BAR**'.
17	LIP	The missing three-letter word from 'S**LIP**PERY' is '**LIP**'.
18	SON	The missing three-letter word from 'SEA**SON**' is '**SON**'.
19	TAG	The missing three-letter word from 'S**TAG**E' is '**TAG**'.
20	OUT	The missing three-letter word from 'S**OUT**H' is '**OUT**'.
21	PAT	The missing three-letter word from '**PAT**IENCE' is '**PAT**'.
22	ADD	The missing three-letter word from 'L**ADD**ER' is '**ADD**'.

VERBAL REASONING: TEST D

Question	Answer	Explanation
23	Romera	**Romera** is the only one who speaks Spanish and Portuguese; therefore, he cannot communicate with the others.
24	**introduce** and **launch**	The two words closest in meaning are '**introduce**' and '**launch**'. Both words are synonyms for 'initiate' and 'instigate'.
25	**fortunate** and **lucky**	The two words closest in meaning are '**fortunate**' and '**lucky**'. Both words are synonyms for 'blessed' and 'advantaged'.
26	**murmur** and **mumble**	The two words closest in meaning are '**murmur**' and '**mumble**'. Both words are synonyms for 'mutter' and 'whisper'.
27	**ponder** and **consider**	The two words closest in meaning are '**ponder**' and '**consider**'. Both words are synonyms for 'review' and 'contemplate'.
28	**zealous** and **enthusiastic**	The two words closest in meaning are '**zealous**' and '**enthusiastic**'. Both words are synonyms for 'passionate' and 'fervent'.
29	**loop** and **coil**	The two words closest in meaning are '**loop**' and '**coil**'. Both words are synonyms for 'bend' and 'curve'.
30	**unusual** and **curious**	The two words closest in meaning are '**unusual**' and '**curious**'. Both words are synonyms for 'strange' and 'odd'.
31	w	Move the letter 'w' to make 'rung' and '**w**heat'.
32	g	Move the letter 'g' to make 'rate' and '**g**rain'.
33	t	Move the letter 't' to make 'hear' and 's**t**age'.
34	u	Move the letter 'u' to make 'bond' and 'bog**u**s'.
35	i	Move the letter 'i' to make 'host' and 'cop**i**ed'.
36	r	Move the letter 'r' to make 'chat' and 'c**r**ave'.
37	v	Move the letter 'v' to make 'shoe' and 'se**v**en'.
38	1954	0 = N, 1 = J, 2 = O, 3 = E, 4 = T, S = 5, 7 = A, 8 = B, and 9 = U. BEAN SOBS JUST 8370 5285 1954 Therefore, the correct code for 'JUST' is **1954**.
39	BANJO	The correct word with the code 87012 is '**BANJO**' *(see code in 38 above)*.
40	82754	The correct code for 'BOAST' is **82754** *(see code in 38 above)*.
41	1539	1 = P, 3 = R, 5 = A, 7 = E, and 9 = T. REAR TRAP PART SPIN 3753 9351 1539 4128 Therefore, the correct code for 'PART' is **1539**.
42	SPIRE	The correct word with the code 41237 is '**SPIRE**' *(see code in 41 above)*.
43	3597	The correct code for 'RATE' is **3597** *(see code in 41 above)*.

VERBAL REASONING: TEST D

Question	Answer	Explanation
44	snow	Let the letters in 'grass' = 12345, then 'grow' = 12 + ow. Likewise, if steal = 12345, then 'stow' = 12 + ow. Therefore, 'snake' (12345) gives **snow** (12 + ow).
45	sold	Let the letters in 'blank' = 12345, then 'bank' = 1345. Likewise, if 'cease' = 12345, then 'case' = 1345. Therefore, 'scold' (12345) gives **sold** (1345).
46	ban	Let the letters in 'these' = 12345, then 'the' = 125. Likewise, if 'faint' = 12345, then 'fat' = 125. Therefore, 'bacon' (12345) gives **ban** (125).
47	late	Let the letters in 'relate' = 123456, then 'tale' = 5432. Likewise, if 'regard' = 123456, then 'rage' = 5432. Therefore, 'metals' (123456) gives **late** (5432).
48	sad	Let the letters in 'blast' = 12345, then 'tab' = 531. Likewise, if 'prior' = 12345, then 'rip' = 531. Therefore, 'draws' (12345) gives **sad** (531).
49	and	Let the letters in 'apple' = 12345, then 'pea' = 351. Likewise, if 'heads' = 12345, then 'ash' = 351. Therefore, 'drawn' (12345) gives **and** (351).
50	meal	Let the letters in 'aware' = 12345, then 'wear' = 2514. Likewise, if 'spite' = 12345, then 'pest' = 2514. Therefore, 'ample' (12345) gives **meal** (2514).
51	36	Looking at each set as (a [b] c), then b = a - c, so the answer is 54 - 18 = **36**.
52	94	Looking at each set as (a [b] c), then b = 2a + c, so the answer is 2 x 19 + 56 = **94**.
53	5	Looking at each set as (a [b] c), then b = c ÷ a, so the answer is 55 ÷ 11 = **5.**
54	56	Looking at each set as (a [b] c), then b = a + c, so the answer is 24 + 32 = **56**.
55	30	Looking at each set as (a [b] c), then b = 2(c - a), so the answer is 2(31 - 16) = **30**.
56	150	Looking at each set as (a [b] c), then b = 2ac, so the answer is 2 x 15 x 5 = **150**.
57	47	Looking at each set as (a [b] c), then b = 3c + a, so the answer is 3 x 14 + 5 = **47**.
58	for miles	The hidden four-letter word is 'form' (**FOR M**iles).
59	hope starting	The hidden four-letter word is 'pest' (ho**PE ST**arting).
60	Doctors aid	The hidden four-letter word is 'said' (Doctor**S AID**).
61	was poorly	The hidden four-letter word is 'wasp' (**WAS P**oorly).
62	natural order	The hidden four-letter word is 'lord' (natura**L ORD**er).
63	ship leaves	The hidden four-letter word is 'plea' (shi**P LEA**ves).
64	never be	The hidden four-letter word is 'verb' (ne**VER B**e).
65	It emits	The hidden four-letter word is 'item' (**IT EM**its).

VERBAL REASONING: TEST D

Question	Answer	Explanation
66	C	Y Y (or 25 miles, 25 miles) L—H (45 miles)
67	season	The word '**season**' can describe the time of year or it can describe the action of putting herbs onto food. The word goes equally well with 'month' / 'time' and 'flavour' / 'spice'.
68	brand	The word '**brand**' can describe marking something or can be the name of a company. The word goes equally well with 'mark' / 'stamp' and 'make' / 'label'.
69	contract	The word '**contract**' can describe decreasing and shortening an object, or it can be a paper or verbal agreement. The word goes equally well with 'shrink' / 'reduce' and 'agreement' / 'document'.
70	root	The word '**root**' can describe the source of something or a part of a plant. The word goes equally well with 'source' / 'origin' and 'stem' / 'leaf'.
71	bolt	The word '**bolt**' can describe fastening a door lock or an arrow shape. The word goes equally well with 'lock' / 'fasten' and 'flash' / 'lightning'.
72	crane	The word '**crane**' can describe stretching out a part of your body (e.g. your head) or a machine uses to hoist items up. The word goes equally well with 'stretch' / 'extend' and 'winch' / 'hoist'.
73	turn	The word '**turn**' can describe physically moving your body in a different direction or transforming something into another thing. The word goes equally well with 'spin' / 'rotate' and 'change' / 'become'.
74	V	The missing letter is 'V'. EAH becomes '**have**' and NREE becomes '**never**'.
75	B	The missing letter is 'B'. ELA becomes '**able**' and MPEROL becomes '**problem**'.
76	K	The missing letter is 'K'. OOGNIL becomes '**looking**' and OCSS becomes '**socks**'.
77	V	The missing letter is 'V'. ISLE becomes '**lives**' and LLGAIE becomes '**village**'.
78	T	The missing letter is 'T'. RAWE becomes '**water**' and NOFE becomes '**often**'.
79	N	The missing letter is 'N'. KIG becomes '**king**' and ROCW becomes '**crown**'.
80	I	The missing letter is 'I'. DMASTU becomes '**stadium**' and CYT becomes '**city**'.

Other Titles in the First Past The Post® Series

Verbal Reasoning: Cloze Tests

Cloze tests are passages with missing words or letters. The student must either select the missing word from a set of several options, or complete the word by filling in the missing letters. This series has been specifically developed to prepare your child for the three styles of cloze test they could face during the exam: Word Bank, Multiple Choice and Partial Words. Each book contains all three question styles as well as full answers and explanations.

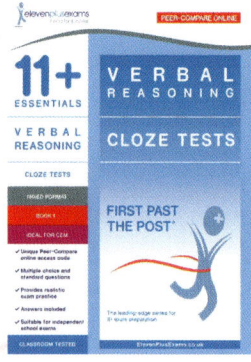

Each book in this series allows access to the Peer-Compare Online system, which assesses the candidate's performance anonymously on a question-by-question basis. This helps identify areas for improvement and benchmarks the candidate's score against that of others who have taken the same tests.

Other Titles in the First Past The Post® Series

Verbal Reasoning: Vocabulary

A good vocabulary is key to success in all 11 plus and Common Entrance exams. All exam boards use questions designed to test the candidates' vocabulary in both the English and Verbal Reasoning sections of contemporary multi-discipline exams. These books have been designed to improve the student's vocabulary through a focus on learning synonyms and antonyms. Each book covers several question styles in order to expose the candidate to as many as possible in readiness for the exam. In each book, there are several timed topic-specific tests and several timed mixed tests, which include several question styles. Full answers and explanations are included.

Each book in this series allows access to the Peer-Compare Online system, which assesses the candidate's performance anonymously on a question-by-question basis. This helps identify areas for improvement and benchmarks the candidate's score against that of others who have taken the same tests.

Other Titles in the First Past The Post® Series

Verbal Reasoning: Vocabulary, Spelling & Grammar

These books have been designed to test and improve the candidate's verbal reasoning skills, especially their working knowledge of grammar and spelling and their vocabulary, which is key to success in all 11 plus and Common Entrance exams. Each book covers a large variety of question styles in order to expose the candidate to as many as possible in readiness for the exam. In each book, there are nine timed tests, each of which focuses on a specific question style, and a timed mixed test, which includes several question styles. Full answers and explanations are included.

Each book in this series allows access to the Peer-Compare Online system, which assesses the candidate's performance anonymously on a question-by-question basis. This helps identify areas for improvement and benchmarks the candidate's score against that of others who have taken the same tests.

Other Titles in the First Past The Post® Series

Verbal Reasoning: Vocabulary in Context

These books provide indispensable practice to help improve crucial comprehension and essential reading skills. Each page contains a short piece of text with five highlighted words, five example sentences with missing words and five definitions. The task is to figure out, using the context of the passage to help, which of the five highlighted words fit in which of the example sentences and which matches up with which definition. These books are not based on an exam-style format, instead they are designed to help build fundamental skills that are key to success in all 11 plus and Common Entrance English and Verbal Reasoning exams. Full answers and explanations are included.

The books in this series come in four levels of difficulty, each level offering more challenging vocabulary than the last, to encourage development of comprehension abilities and confidence. Level 1 is the easiest, and Level 4 is the hardest.

Other Titles in the First Past The Post® Series

Verbal Reasoning: Puzzles

This puzzle series aims to test and improve the candidate's vocabulary in a fun and engaging way. A wide vocabulary is at the heart of all 11 plus and Common Entrance exams, and many question styles in the English and Verbal Reasoning sections are designed to test this. These books are filled with challenging crosswords and word searches which test over 700 synonyms, antonyms and homophones. Whilst being engaged in a fun activity, the candidate will widen their vocabulary with a selection of useful new words.

Each book in this series contains puzzles which focus on each of synonyms, antonyms and homophones. Within each word group, there are puzzles at three difficulty levels. The final four puzzles on each topic are mixed puzzles, which feature all three word groups. It is easy to monitor progress and pinpoint areas for improvement with progress charts and word jotters.

Other Titles in the First Past The Post® Series

Mathematics: Practice Papers (GL)

These books provide real exam practice via four timed tests. These are tailored towards the Granada Learning (GL) Mathematics assessments but provide invaluable practice for all exam boards. Each test covers a large range of topics so that, over the four papers, all known maths topics that are likely to come up in the real GL exam are covered. The structure of each test is designed to reflect the likely make-up of the real exam. . Full answers and explanations are included.

Each test can be marked and evaluated via our Peer-Compare Online system, which assesses the candidate's performance anonymously on a question-by-question basis. This helps identify areas for improvement and benchmarks the candidate's score against that of others who have taken the same tests.

Other Titles in the First Past The Post® Series

English: Practice Papers (GL)

These books provide real exam practice via four timed tests. These are tailored towards the Granada Learning (GL) English assessments but provide invaluable practice for all exam boards. Each test comprises a comprehension section and a spelling, punctuation and grammar section, reflecting the likely make-up of the real exam. Full answers and explanations are included.

Each test can be marked and evaluated via our Peer-Compare Online system, which assesses the candidate's performance anonymously on a question-by-question basis. This helps identify areas for improvement and benchmarks the candidate's score against that of others who have taken the same tests.